EAST HAM

The
ANTISLAVERY
MOVEMENT

SOCIAL REFORM MOVEMENTS

The

ANTISLAVERY MOVEMENT

JAMES T. ROGERS

Facts On File®

AN INFOBASE HOLDINGS COMPANY

The Antislavery Movement

Copyright © 1994 by James T. Rogers

Facts On File, Inc.
460 Park Avenue South
New York NY 10016

Library of Congress Cataloging-in-Publication Data
Rogers, James T.
    The antislavery movement / James T. Rogers.
      p. cm. — (Social reform movements series)
    Includes bibliographical references and index.
    ISBN 0-8160-2907-5
    1. Slavery—United States—Anti-slavery movements—Juvenile literature. 2. Abolitionists—United States—History—19th century—Juvenile literature. 3. Slaves—United States—Emancipation—Juvenile literature. 4. Afro-Americans—History—To 1863—Juvenile literature. 5. Afro-Americans—History—1863–1877—Juvenile literature. [1. Slavery—Anti-slavery movements. 2. Afro-Americans—History. 3. Afro-Americans—Civil rights.] I. Title. II. Series.
    E449.R724 1994   93–40960
    973'.0496073—dc20
All photographs courtesy of the Library of Congress.

Text design by Fred Pusterla
Cover design by Nora Wertz
Printed in the United States of America

MP FOF 10 9 8 7 6 5 4 3 2 1

C O N T E N T S

P R O L O G U E

The following advertisement, placed by the sheriff of Newton County, Georgia, appeared in the *Milledgeville Southern Recorder* on January 7, 1851:

> *Will be sold before the Court-house door in the town of Covington, within the usual hours of sale, on the first Tuesday in February next, the following property, to wit: Three Negroes—John, a boy about 18 years old; Ann, a girl about 4 years old; Riley, a boy about three years old; all levied on as the property of Burwell Moss, to satisfy a mortgage. . . .*

Southern newspapers were full of similar advertisements in the years before the Civil War. Several things about the wording of this one are noteworthy. John, Ann and Riley are "property." That was the legal status of slaves in the antebellum South—in a class with land and cattle, bought and sold without consideration for anything but the economics of the transaction. These three pieces of property are "Negroes." All American slaves were Negroes, and most Negroes in the South were slaves. John, Ann and Riley are children. Although the advertisement does not say so, they were probably being sold away from their parents, or perhaps the parents had already been sold away from them. Such a tearing apart of families happened frequently during the slave era. John, Ann and Riley are identified only by their first names. That is the way slaves were typically known in the South. If a last name was accorded to a slave, it was usually the surname of the owner.

Looking back almost 130 years to the abolition of slavery after a bitter and bloody war, it is difficult to believe that human beings could have been treated in this way. Yet slavery was a pillar of the agricultural economy of the South. It was taken for granted by most white Southerners and fiercely defended by them, to the point of suppressing freedom of speech and the press and of inflicting actual violence against people who opposed what was known in those days as "the peculiar institution at the South."

A slave auction was depicted in *Harper's Weekly* in 1861. Prospective buyers are grouped to the left and right in front of the platform holding the slaves. One buyer is on the platform examining a slave's chest. On the right side of the platform the auctioneer calls for bids on a slave mother and her infant.

("Peculiar" in this expression meant "distinctive" or "characteristic" rather than the more common meaning today of "eccentric" or "odd.")

Yet the abolition of slavery at the end of the Civil War in 1865 would be only the middle of the story of the antislavery movement. The legacy of slavery continued for decades and indeed remains in the form of various kinds of discrimination against blacks, notwithstanding the achievements of the civil rights movement over the past 40 years. For many years after the Civil War, large numbers of blacks in the South continued in agricultural work under conditions hardly better than slavery. Freedom brought them wages for their work, but meager ones, and often they saw little of the money because employers charged them for food, housing and supplies. Laws and practices in the South excluded them from voting, and regulated their behavior closely. They were kept in segregated schools that received far less money than was provided for the schools attended by white children.

Thousands of blacks migrated from the South after the Civil War, only to find that life was not a great deal better for them in the North. There, too, they faced discrimination in housing, education and job opportunities. They were sometimes attacked by whites. Even the U.S. government discriminated against blacks, keeping them in segregated military units throughout World War I (1914–1918) and most of World War II (1939–1945).

The antislavery movement, regarded as an effort not only to abolish slavery but also to erase its aftereffects, therefore did not end with the legal ending of slavery in 1865 under the terms of the 13th Amendment to the U.S. Constitution, which says: "Neither slavery nor involuntary servitude, except as a punishment for crime whereof the party shall have been duly convicted, shall exist within the United States or any place subject to their jurisdiction." The pages that follow describe the antislavery movement, beginning with the conditions of slavery that brought the movement into being and carrying the story up to the period after World War II when civil rights laws with teeth in them began to bring about some real improvements in the conditions faced by blacks and the opportunities open to them.

PROLOGUE NOTE

page vi   "Will be sold . . . " Quoted in *Kenneth M. Stampp,* **The Peculiar Institution,** p. 200–201.

The
ANTISLAVERY
MOVEMENT

CHAPTER One

SLAVERY
A Life in Misery

The "peculiar institution" did not begin as slavery. In 1619 John Rolfe, secretary and recorder of the British colony of Virginia (much of which is now the state of Virginia), reported that "about the last of August there came to Virginia a Dutch man of warre that sold us twenty negers." The ship's captain sold those 20 blacks from Africa as indentured servants, which is how they and other blacks were treated for several decades. An indentured servant could expect to be given his freedom after he had worked for a certain number of years (usually seven) to pay off the debt incurred by the person who had bought his services. Indeed, the sketchy records show that at least one of the men on that first ship did quite well for himself after receiving his freedom. Anthony Johnson was freed after a few years of indentured work. He bought land, became wealthy and eventually had some indentured Africans of his own.

Before long, however, the black—unlike the white indentured servant—came to be regarded as being in bondage to his purchaser for life. He was, in short, a slave. Virginia legalized slavery in 1661.

One wonders why indentured blacks were forced into slavery and indentured whites were not. The explanation is a complicated one. Blacks were pagans from a faraway land. A white was "one of us." Blacks looked and seemed strange to whites, who regarded them as childlike and easily bossed. Whites in the South gradually came to believe they were actually doing the best thing for Negroes by making them slaves. James H. Hammond, a slave owner who was governor of South Carolina for a time before the Civil War, said that slavery provided for the white man the only basis on which he could do something for a group of "hopelessly and permanently inferior" people. (His state, in a code of 1712 on the treatment of slaves, held that blacks are "of barbarous, wild, savage natures" and must be governed by such special laws "as may restrain the disorders, rapines and inhumanity to which they are naturally prone.") Hammond also had some thoughts about what slavery did for the whites. It had enabled them to tame the southern wilderness and turn it into an agricultural wonderland. Moreover, slaves gave their owner the leisure to cultivate his mind and to help create in the South what was, in Hammond's view, a society notable for its culture and gentility. Slavery was "the greatest of all the great blessings which a kind providence has bestowed."

One wonders, too, why African tribes let their people be taken into slavery. The reason was money. A trader—usually from England, Holland or France—would appear, telling the tribal chief or king that he was prepared to pay for people to be taken into slavery. The trader and the king would bargain until an agreement was reached on price. The king would then put the matter in the hands of assistants whose job was to find and round up natives who suited the trader. Those unfortunate people would be marched to the trader's ship—in chains, for they did not go willingly.

Then began what the American historian John Hope Franklin has called "a veritable nightmare," the voyage across the Atlantic to the New World. It was called the "middle passage" because it was the middle part of the journey that began in Africa and ended in slavery in America. The ships transporting the slaves were grossly overcrowded; the more slaves the trader could pack in, the more profits he could make when the ship reached its destination and he sold them. Chained together in pairs, the slaves hardly had room to lie down.

A man who went through this ordeal as a child later wrote about it. In Nigeria, his native land, he was Olaudah Equiano. Kidnapped in 1756 at the age of 11, he survived the middle passage and was sold to a ship's captain, who renamed him Gustavus Vassa. He was sold and resold, eventually to a kindly merchant in Philadelphia who allowed him to save enough money to buy his freedom. In 1789 he wrote a two-volume account of his experiences, *The Interesting Narrative of the Life of Olaudah Equiano, or Gustavus Vassa, the African, Written by Himself.* Describing the middle passage, he said:

> *The shrieks of the women, and the groans of the dying, rendered the whole a scene of horror almost inconceivable. . . .One day, when we had a smooth sea and moderate wind, two of my wearied countrymen who were chained together . . . preferring death to such a life of misery, somehow made it through the nettings and jumped into the sea: immediately another quite dejected fellow, who on account of his illness was suffered to be out of irons, also followed their example; and I believe many more would very soon have done the same, if they had not been prevented by the ship's crew, who were instantly alarmed. Those of us that were the most active, were in a moment put down under the deck, and there was such a noise and confusion amongst the people of the ship as I never heard before, to stop her, and to get the boat out to go after the slaves. However two of the*

The transport of slaves from Africa to North America was called the middle passage because it was the middle stage between freedom in Africa and the auction block in America. The conditions of the trip were miserable, as indicated by this scene of the hold of the slave ship *Gloria*.

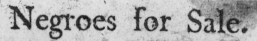

Negroes for Sale.

A Cargo of very fine stout Men and Women, in good order and fit for immediate service, just imported from the Windward Coast of Africa, in the Ship Two Brothers.——

Conditions are one half Cash or Produce, the other half payable the first of January next, giving Bond and Security if required.

The Sale to be opened at 10 o'Clock each Day, in Mr. Bourdeaux's Yard, at No, 48, on the Bay.

May 19, 1784. JOHN MITCHELL.

Thirty Seasoned Negroes

To be Sold for Credit, at Private Sale.

AMONGST which is a Carpenter, none of whom are known to be dishonest.

Also, to be sold for Cash, a regular bred young Negroe Man-Cook, born in this Country, who served several Years under an exceeding good French Cook abroad, and his Wife a middle aged Washer-Woman, (both very honest) and their two Children. *Likewise,* a young Man a Carpenter. For Terms apply to the Printer.

Advertisements for the sale of slaves were common on billboards and in newspapers during the slavery era. These two date from the late 18th century.

wretches were drowned, but they got the other, and afterwards flogged him unmercifully, for thus attempting to prefer death to slavery. In this manner we continued to undergo more hardships than I can now relate, hardships which are inseparable from this accursed trade. Many a time we were near suffocation from the want of fresh air.

This and the stench of the necessary tubs [serving as toilets] carried off many.

For those who survived the middle passage—and there were many who did not—it was off the ship and onto the auction block at the end of the voyage. Buyers at a slave auction were much like buyers at a horse auction today. They felt muscles, looked at teeth and paid the most for the healthiest looking specimens.

Such a scene was described in 1853 by Solomon Northup, a free black who was kidnapped and sold into slavery. It was 12 years before he regained his freedom. The auction in which he was sold took place in New Orleans in 1841. He wrote of it in *Twelve Years a Slave:*

> *Many customers called to examine Freeman's "new lot." [Theophilus Freeman owned the auction business.] The latter gentleman was very loquacious, dwelling at much length upon our several good points and qualities. He would make us hold up our heads, walk briskly back and forth, while customers would feel of our hands and arms and bodies, turn us about, ask us what we could do, make us open our mouths and show our teeth, precisely as a jockey examines a horse which he is about to barter for or purchase. Sometimes a man or woman was taken back to the small house in the yard, stripped, and inspected more minutely. Scars upon a slave's back were considered evidence of a rebellious or unruly spirit, and hurt his sale.*

Northup told of a scene at the same auction involving a slave named Eliza and her children, Emily and Randall. A buyer had shown an interest in acquiring Randall:

> *The little fellow was made to jump, and run across the floor, and perform many other feats, exhibiting his activity and condition. All the time the trade was going on, Eliza was crying aloud, and wringing her hands. She besought the man not to buy him, unless he also bought herself and Emily. She promised, in that case, to be the most faithful slave that ever lived. The man answered that he could not afford it, and then Eliza burst into a paroxysm of grief, weeping plaintively. Freeman turned round to her, savagely, with his whip in his uplifted hand,*

*ordering her to stop her noise, or he would flog her. . . .
Eliza shrunk before him, and tried to wipe away her
tears, but it was all in vain. She wanted to be with her
children, she said, the little time she had to live. All the
frowns and threats of Freeman, could not wholly silence
the afflicted mother. She kept on begging and beseeching
them, most piteously, not to separate the three. Over and
over again she told them how she loved her boy. . . .
But it was of no avail; the man could not afford it. The
bargain was agreed upon, and Randall must go alone.
Then Eliza ran to him; embraced him passionately; kissed
him again and again; told him to remember her—all the
while her tears falling into the boy's face like rain. . . .
The planter from Baton Rouge, with his new
purchase, was ready to depart.
"Don't cry, mama. I will be a good boy. Don't cry,"
said Randall, looking back, as they passed out the door.
What has become of the lad, God knows. It was a
mournful scene indeed. I would have cried myself if I
had dared.*

The prices paid for slaves increased steadily as slavery became more entrenched. Early in the 19th century, a good field hand fetched about $350 in Virginia and $500 in Louisiana. By 1860, a prime field hand went for $1,000 in Virginia and $1,500 in Louisiana.

Put to work, usually on a farm, the slave led a rigidly controlled life. A workday of 15 hours in the fields, six days a week, was standard. On a farm with few slaves, the slaves provided labor in addition to field work, and the master often worked with them. On plantations with 30 slaves or more, the work tended to be specialized and was likely to be bossed by a hired overseer, perhaps with help from some of the more trusted slaves. The plantation drew a distinction between household servants and field hands. In the household, slaves served as butlers, cooks, coachmen, laundresses, seamstresses, housemaids, chambermaids, nannies and personal servants to members of the slave-owning family. In the field, the specialized jobs included driving wagons, ditching, tending livestock and making or repairing equipment.

Frederick Douglass, a slave in Maryland who escaped to freedom in 1838 and became a prominent and highly impressive

ousing was poorly built, cramped, dirty and meagerly
One planter in Mississippi had 24 huts, each measuring
et, for his 150 slaves.

conditions made for much sickness, as Southern doctors
inually telling slave owners. A physician in Alabama
he *Southern Cultivator* in 1850: "One of the most prolific
of disease among negroes is the condition of their
. . Small, low, tight and filthy; their houses can be but
ies of disease." Hammond, looking at the situation as a
ner, said: "All the plagues of Egypt still infest these
. I don't believe there is a disease to which the human
s subject that is not to be seen here in the run of the
The fact is my negroes decrease . . . and I am hampered
med beyond endurance by sickness."

uld hardly be expected that slaves would work any harder
ey had to under these harsh conditions. *De Bow's Review*
d in 1849: "Every attempt to force a slave beyond the limit
fixes himself as a sufficient amount of labor to render his
, instead of extorting more work, only tends to make him
itable, unmanageable, a vexation and a curse. If you pro-
is regular hours of labor, his movements become propor-
y slower." A planter in Virginia wrote: "The most general
in the character of the negro, is hypocrisy; and this hypoc-
equently makes him pretend to more ignorance than he
sses; and if his master treats him as a fool, he will be sure to
e fool's part. This is a very convenient trait, as it frequently
s as an apology for awkwardness and neglect of duty."

he slave also exacted revenge from being careless in his work.
ow's Review printed in 1851 a letter from Dr. Samuel A.
wright of Louisiana complaining of the slave's habit of doing
ork "in a headlong, careless manner, treading down with his
or cutting with his hoe" the crops he was supposed to culti-
, breaking his tools and "spoiling everything."

Because of these tendencies, slave owners were much con-
ed about disciplining slaves. Charles Pettigrew, a planter and
e owner in North Carolina, stated the situation in 1802: "It is
ty, that agreeable to the nature of things Slavery and Tyranny
st go together and that there is no such thing as having an
dient and useful Slave, without the painful exercise of undue

speaker at abolitionist meetings
treatment at the hands of the ill-t[…]
Auld regarded Douglass as rebell[…]
"slave breaker," Edward Covey. D[…]

> *I remained with Mr. Covey one ye[…]*
> *six months that I was there I was w[…]*
> *or cow-skins, every week. Aching [—]*
> *were my constant companions. Fre[…]*
> *used, Mr. Covey thought less of it a[s]*
> *down my spirit than that of hard anc[…]*

Solomon Northup wrote about w[…]
tion. "The hands are required to be in [—]
it is light in the morning," he said, "anc[…]
or fifteen minutes, which is given them[…]
allowance of cold bacon, they are not p[…]
idle until it is too dark to see, and when tl[…]
times labor until the middle of the night.

The midday meal of cold bacon on tl[…]
was standard fare. A typical weekly food a[…]
a peck of cornmeal and three or four poun[…]
Fruit, vegetables, milk, eggs and fresh m[…]
cases unheard of. It was a diet that provide[…]
badly unbalanced—a situation that was du[…]
to the owner's desire to feed his slaves chea[…]
knowledge at the time of good nutrition.

Cheap, poorly made and required to last[…]
the clothing provided to slaves. James H. [H.]
manual for the management of the slaves[…]
Plantation on the Savannah River in South Ca[…]
it said: "Each man gets in the fall 2 shirts of co[…]
of woolen pants and a woolen jacket. In the sprii[…]
shirting and 2 pr. of cotton pants. . . . Each wori[…]
of shoes every fall, and a heavy blanket every thii[…]
as hard as they did, the slaves had little time to cl[…]
clothes, which came to look tattered long befoi[…]
ment. People who visited plantations often con[…]
shabby appearance of the slaves.

Slave l[…]
furnished[…]
16 by 14 f[…]
These[…]
were con[…]
wrote in […]
sources[…]
houses. .[…]
laborato[…]
slave ov[…]
Negroes[…]
family i[…]
year. . . .[…]
and alai[…]
It co[…]
than th[…]
reporte[…]
that he[…]
master[…]
unpro[…]
tract h[…]
tionall[…]
defect[…]
risy f[…]
posse[…]
act th[…]
serve[…]
T[…]
De B[…]
Cart[…]
his v[…]
feet[…]
vate[…]
cer[…]
sla[…]
a p[…]
mu[…]
ob[…]

and tyrannical authority." The laws of the slave states recognized this relation and gave masters almost total authority over slaves. A master might get in trouble with the law if he killed or maimed a slave, but otherwise he had free rein.

The lighter penalties included short rations and extra work, as on Sundays and holidays when other slaves were excused. A more severe penalty was to put a misbehaving slave in the stocks, the wooden device with holes where a man's feet or feet and hands could be locked. Thomas Affleck, author of the widely used *Cotton Plantation Record and Account Book*, called the stocks an appropriate punishment. "So secured, in a lonely, quiet place, where no communication can be held with anyone, nothing but bread and water allowed, and the confinement extending from Saturday, when they drop work, until Sabbath evening," he wrote, a slave will be effectively punished. The severest punishment was whipping. Few grown slaves escaped it. James Hammond had advice on this subject: "The highest punishment must not exceed 100 lashes in one day and to that extent only in extreme cases. In general, 15 to 20 lashes will be a sufficient flogging."

The master's authority was backed up by his state's slave code. Every slave state had one. The codes defined the property rights of owners in regard to their slaves and required slaves to submit to their masters and respect all white people. A slave could not be away from his owner's property without a pass. No more than five slaves could assemble away from home unless a white was present to make sure that no rebellion was being planned. No one was allowed to teach a slave to read or write. The Louisiana code of 1806 summarized the position: "The condition of the slave being merely a passive one, his submission to his master and all who represent him is not susceptible of modification or restriction. . . . He owes to his master, and to all his family, a respect without bounds, and an absolute obedience."

Frederick Douglass was as a child owned for a time by Hugh Auld and lived with his family in Baltimore. Mrs. Auld, a kindly woman, undertook to teach Douglass to read. Douglass later described her husband's reaction when he found out:

> Master Hugh was astounded beyond measure, and, probably for the first time, proceeded to unfold to his

*wife the true philosophy of the slave system, and the
peculiar rules necessary in the nature of the case to be
observed in the management of human chattels. Of
course he forbade her to give me any further instruction,
telling her that to do so was in the first place unlawful,
as it was also unsafe; "for," said he, "if you give a nigger
an inch he will take an ell [an old standard measure
amounting to 45 inches]. Learning will spoil the best
nigger in the world. If he learns to read the Bible, it will
forever unfit him to be a slave. He should know nothing
but the will of his master, and learn to obey it."*

It is small wonder that many of the slaves facing these hard
conditions tried to run away. Fugitive slaves were a constant
problem for slave owners.

Their militant efforts to recapture fugitives, even those who
had escaped to free states or to Canada, played an important part
in the growing friction between South and North in the first 60
years of the 19th century. Many whites made a living as slave
catchers, even in the North. F. H. Pettis, a lawyer in New York,
advertised in Southern newspapers that he had much experience
"in causing fugitive slaves to be secured . . . in defiance of the
Abolitionists." Gustavus A. Henry, a slave owner in Mississippi,
described the talents of a slave catcher in his employ: "He follows
a negro with his dogs . . . and never fails to overtake him. It is his
profession and he makes some $600 per annum by it."

Life from the fugitive's point of view was described in 1864 by
Octave Johnson, who had escaped from his owner in 1862 and
eventually became a corporal in the Union army:

*I was born in New Orleans; I am 23 years of age; I was
raised by Arthur Thiboux of New Orleans; I am by trade
a cooper; I was treated pretty well at home; in 1855
master sold my mother; and in 1861 he sold me to S.
Contrell of St. James Parish for $2,400; here I worked by
task [an assigned amount of work per day] at my trade;
one morning the bell was rung for us to go to work so
early that I could not see, and I lay still, because I was
working by task; for this the overseer was going to have
me whipped, and I ran away to the woods, where I
remained for a year and a half; I had to steal my food;
took turkeys, chickens and pigs; before I left our number*

had increased to thirty, of whom ten were women; we
were four miles in the rear of the plantation house;
sometimes we would rope beef cattle and drag them
out to our hiding place; we obtained matches from
our friends on the plantation; we slept on logs and
burned cypress leaves to make a smoke and keep away
mosquitoes; Eugene Jardeau, master of hounds, hunted us
for three months; often those at work [on the plantation]
would betray those in the swamp, for fear of being
implicated in their escape; we furnished meat to our
fellow-servants in the field, who would return corn meal;
one day twenty hounds came after me; I called the party
to my assistance and we killed eight of the bloodhounds;
then we all jumped into Bayou Faupron; the dogs
followed us and the alligators caught six of them; "the
alligators preferred dog flesh to personal flesh;" we
escaped and came to Camp Parapet [a Union army
encampment], where I was first employed in the
Commissary's office, then as a servant to Col. Hanks;
then I joined his regiment.

From the earliest days, some slaves tried to win their freedom
by appealing to the authorities. A typical petition came from a
group of slaves to the Massachusetts General Court in 1777. (One
should remember in reading it that spelling and capitalization
were unsettled in the 18th century and, additionally, that these
petitioners were slaves with little experience in reading and writing.) The petition said in part:

The petition of A Great Number of Blackes detained in
a State of slavery in the Bowels of a free & Christian
Country Humbly sheweth that your Petitioners appre-
hend that they have in Common with all other men a
Natural and Unaliable Right to that freedom which the
Grat Parent of the Unavers hath Bestowed equalley on
all menkind and which they have Never forfeited by any
Compact or agreement whatever—but that wher Unjustly
Dragged by the hand of cruel Power from their Derest
friends and sum of them Even torn from the Embraces
of their tender Parents—from A populous Pleasant and
plentiful country and in violation of the Laws of Nature
and off Nations and in defiance of all the tender feelings
of humanity Brough hear Either to Be sold Like Beast
of Burthen & Like them Condemnd to Slavery for

Life—Among A People Profesing the mild Religion of Jesus . . . your honouer Need not to be informed that a Live of Slavery Like that of your petioners Deprived of Every thing Requisit to Render Life Tolable is far worse than Nonexistence.

A similar petition by a group of slaves in Connecticut to the state's General Assembly in 1779 made an additional point. Slavery was bad enough, they said, but "the Perpetrators of this horrid Wickedness . . . have added another dreadful Evil, that of holding us in gross Ignorance."

Some recently freed blacks in Dartmouth, Mass., made the point that even in freedom they faced inequality: they had to pay taxes but, unlike free white men, they could not vote. In 1780 they raised the point in a petition to the legislature:

The petition of several poor Negroes & molattoes who are Inhabitant of the Town of Dartmouth Humbly Sheweth—That we being Chiefly of the African Extract and by Reason of Long Bondag and hard Slavery we have been deprived of Injoying the Profits of our Labouer or the advantage of Inheriting Estates from our Parents as our Neighbouers the white peopel do having some of us not long Injoyed our own Freedom & yet of late, Contrary to the invariable Custom & Practice of the Country we have been & now are Taxed both in our Polls and that small Pittance of Estate which through much hard Labour & Industry we have got together to Sustain our selves & families.

The argument found sympathetic ears. Three years later a state court ruled that black people required to pay taxes were entitled to vote.

Another miserable part of slave life was the frequent break-up of families as owners sold away one member and kept the others, or sold all the members of the family to different buyers. John Q. A. Dennis described the pain of this treatment in a letter that he wrote to Secretary of War Edwin M. Stanton in 1864:

Dear Sir: I am Glad that I have the Honour to Write you afew line I have been in troble for about four yars my Dear wife was taken from me Nov 19th 1859 and left me with three Children and I being a Slave At the time Could Not do Anny thing for the poor little Children for my master it was took me Carry me some forty mile from them So I Could not do for them and the man that they live with half feed them and half Cloth them & beat them like dogs & when I was admited to go to see them it use to brake my heart & Now I say agian I am Glad to have the honour to write you to see if you Can Do Anny thing for me or for my poor little Children I was keap in Slavy untell last Novr 1863. then the Good lord sent the Cornel borne [apparently a Union colonel] Down their in Marland in worsester Co So as I have been recently freed I have but letle to live on but I am Striveing Dear Sir but what I want to know of you Sir is is it possible for me to go & take my Children from those men that keep them in Savery if it is possible will you pleas give me a permit from your hand then I think they would let them go

Dennis asked Stanton to "please excuse my Miserable writeing & answer me as soon as you can." The records do not show whether Stanton or anyone else in the War Department replied.

Sarah Jackson, a slave who succeeded in escaping to freedom in Canada, summed up in a sentence what drove her and so many others to flee their miserable existence. "It is a great heaviness on a person's mind to be a slave."

CHAPTER ONE NOTES

page 1   "about the last of August . . . " Quoted in *Maurice R. Davie*, **Negroes in American Society.** New York: Whittlesey House, 1949, p. 17.

page 2   "hopelessly and permanently . . . " Quoted in *John Hope Franklin*, **The Militant South** (third edition, 1968), p. 83.

page 2   "of barbarous . . . " Quoted in *Kenneth M. Stampp*, **The Peculiar Institution,** p. 11.

page 2   "the greatest of all the great blessings . . . " Quoted in *John Hope Franklin*, **The Militant South,** p. 83.

page 2   "a veritable nightmare . . ." John Hope Franklin, **From Slavery to Freedom,** p. 56.

page 3   "The shrieks . . . " *Paul Edwards* (editor), **Equiano's Travels.** London: Heinemann, 1967, p. 29.

page 5   "Many customers called . . . " Quoted in *Herbert Aptheker* (editor), **A Documentary History of the Negro People in the United States,** vol. 1, p. 207.

page 5   "The little fellow . . . " Quoted in *Herbert Aptheker* (editor), **A Documentary History of the Negro People in the United States,** vol. 1, p. 207.

page 7   "I remained with Mr. Covey . . . " *Frederick Douglass,* **Life and Times of Frederick Douglass.** Boston: De Wolfe & Fiske Co., 1892, p. 148.

page 7   "The hands . . . " Quoted in *Kenneth M. Stampp,* **The Peculiar Institution,** p. 74.

page 7   "Each man gets . . . " Quoted in *Kenneth M. Stampp,* **The Peculiar Institution,** p. 291.

page 8   "One of the most prolific sources . . . " Quoted in *Kenneth M. Stampp,* **The Peculiar Institution,** p. 294.

page 8   "All the plagues . . . " Quoted in *Kenneth M. Stampp,* **The Peculiar Institution,** p. 298.

page 8   "Every attempt . . . " Quoted in *Kenneth M. Stampp,* **The Peculiar Institution,** p. 101.

page 8   "The most general defect . . . " Quoted in *Kenneth M. Stampp,* **The Peculiar Institution,** p. 99.

page 8   "in a headlong . . . " Quoted in *Kenneth M. Stampp,* **The Peculiar Institution,** p. 102.

page 8   "It is a pity . . . " Quoted in *Kenneth M. Stampp*, **The Peculiar Institution,** p. 141.

page 9   "So secured . . . " Quoted in *Kenneth M. Stampp*, **The Peculiar Institution,** p. 173.

page 9   "The highest punishment . . . " Quoted in *Kenneth M. Stampp*, **The Peculiar Institution,** p. 175.

page 9   "The condition of the slave . . . " Quoted in *Kenneth M. Stampp*, **The Peculiar Institution,** p. 207.

page 9   "Master Hugh . . . " *Frederick Douglass*, **Life and Times of Frederick Douglass,** p. 94.

page 10   "in causing fugitive slaves . . . " Quoted in *Kenneth M. Stampp*, **The Peculiar Institution,** p. 153.

page 10   "He follows . . . " Quoted in *Kenneth M. Stampp*, **The Peculiar Institution,** p. 189.

page 10   "I was born . . . " Quoted in *Ira Berlin*, et al. (editors), **Free at Last,** p. 49.

page 11   "The petition of A Great Number of Blackes . . . " Quoted in *Herbert Aptheker* (editor), **A Documentary History of the Negro People in the United States,** vol. 1, p. 9.

page 12   "the Perpetrators . . . " Quoted in *Herbert Aptheker* (editor), **A Documentary History of the Negro People in the United States,** vol. 1, p. 11.

page 12   "The petition of several poor Negroes . . . " Quoted in *Herbert Aptheker* (editor), **A Documentary History of the Negro People in the United States,** vol. 1, p. 15.

page 12   "Dear Sir: . . . " Quoted in *Ira Berlin*, et al. (editors), **Free at Last,** p. 120.

page 13　　"please excuse . . . " Quoted in *Ira Berlin*, et al. (editors), **Free at Last,** p. 121.

page 13　　"It is a great heaviness . . . " *Benjamin Drew,* **The Refugee: or the Narratives of Fugitive Slaves in Canada.** Boston: J. P. Jewett Co., 1856, p. 179.

CHAPTER TWO

STIRRINGS AGAINST SLAVERY
The Beginning of the Abolitionist Movement

Slavery became an entrenched institution in the South little step by little step. The antislavery movement proceeded in the same way. Frederick Douglass, the former slave who became a powerful spokesman for the abolitionists, put it this way:

> No one can tell the day of the month, or the month of the year, upon which slavery was abolished in the United States. We cannot tell even when it began to be abolished. Like the movement of the sea, no man can tell where one wave begins and another ends. The chains of slavery with us were loosened by degrees.

Actually, the United States was somewhat late in joining what had become a worldwide movement for the abolition of slavery. In England, the institution came under attack in the 18th century by such prominent thinkers and writers as John Locke, Daniel Defoe, Alexander Pope, Adam Smith, Thomas Paine and John Wesley. The Society of Friends—the Quakers—became in 1784 the first group to petition Parliament for the abolition of slavery. Pressure increased a few years later with the formation of the Society for the Abolition of the Slave Trade. Parliament responded by putting an end to the slave trade in 1808; in 1838 it abolished slavery on all British territory. Other European nations took similar steps during this period. The newly independent nations in South America—Chile, Colombia, Bolivia, Guatemala, Mexico, Uruguay, Argentina and Peru—had all abolished slavery by 1854.

In the United States, the antislavery movement was mostly the work of individuals until late in the 18th century. Gustavus Vassa, in his autobiography of 1789, voiced the sentiment that gave the movement its increasing force. Addressing the owners of slaves and the people of the North and South who did not own slaves but tolerated slavery, he said:

> O, ye nominal Christians! might not an African ask you, Learned you this from your God who says unto you, Do unto all men as you would men should do unto you? Is it not enough that we are torn from our country and friends, to toil for your luxury and lust and gain? . . . Why are parents to lose their children, brothers their sisters, or husbands their wives? Surely, this is a new refinement in cruelty which . . . adds fresh horrors even to the wretchedness of slavery.

Vassa was not alone. Many people in the North and South, particularly those who took their religion seriously, saw slavery as an evil. The Quakers especially viewed slavery as violating the teachings of the Bible, and it was a Quaker group in Germantown, Pennsylvania, that in 1688 issued the first known American protest against slavery. Just as Vassa did a century later, they called attention to the Golden Rule "that we should do to all men as we would be done to ourselves." And, they asked, "what thing in the world can be done worse toward us, than if men should rob or steal us away and sell us for slaves to strange countries?"

It was the Quakers of Pennsylvania who organized America's first antislavery society in 1775. A similar group today would probably have a short and easy-to-remember name, but theirs was very long: The Pennsylvania Society for Promoting the Abolition of Slavery, the Relief of Free Negroes Unlawfully Held in Bondage, and for Improving the Condition of the African Race. Benjamin Franklin, who had urged his fellow Quakers to form the society, became its first president.

Another famous person of the time appeared to be of two minds about slavery. Thomas Jefferson owned slaves, but in writing the Declaration of Independence he included a section opposing slavery. The Declaration directs a series of charges against King George III of England, citing them as reasons why the American colonies are announcing their independence. One of the charges originally in the Declaration condemned the king for tolerating if not encouraging slavery. "He has waged cruel war against human nature itself," the clause said, "violating its most sacred rights of life and liberty in the persons of a distant people who never offended him, captivating and carrying them into slavery in another hemisphere or to incur miserable death in their transportation thither." This clause was taken out of the Declaration because of opposition from the delegates of Georgia and South Carolina to the Second Continental Congress, which had called for the Declaration to be written. Some of the delegates from the North opposed the clause, too; of them, Jefferson said that "tho' their people have very few slaves themselves, yet they had been pretty considerable carriers of them to others."

Jefferson also had a hand in writing what became the Ordinance of 1787, passed by the Continental Congress. As Jefferson wrote it, slavery would be prohibited in all new territories acquired by the new United States. Proslavery forces again brought about a change, which limited the ban on slavery to the Northwest Territory—what is now the heart of the Midwest, consisting of the states of Ohio, Indiana, Illinois, Wisconsin and most of Michigan. Nonetheless, it was a huge area closed to slavery, and as its population grew it became a bulwark of the nation's progress toward freedom and individual liberty.

Jefferson and Franklin were among many prominent Americans who spoke out against slavery. Others included John Jay, the first chief justice of the United States, who helped found the New York Society for Promoting the Manumission [freeing] of Slaves and served as its first president. Benjamin Rush, a physician and signer of the Declaration of Independence, published several pamphlets against slavery.

Many slave owners had a bad conscience about slavery and responded by freeing their slaves in the act called manumission (from the Latin words for "hand" and "let go"). Other slaves were able to buy their freedom. They were usually the ones who had some skill as craftsmen or mechanics and could earn money by working at times for people other than their masters. And from the earliest days of slavery there was a steady flow of slaves who simply fled to freedom in the North. By 1790, according to the first U.S. census, there were 59,557 free blacks in the country—7.9 percent of the total black population of 757,181.

Whatever their method of gaining freedom, the free blacks seldom enjoyed all the rights that white citizens took for granted. They often had to have passes to move about, they lacked standing in the courts comparable to that of whites and they usually could not meet the property and educational qualifications required of voters. They also were in real danger of being captured or kidnapped and returned to slavery. Three free black men in Boston were kidnapped in 1788 and sold into slavery in the French colony of Martinique. Even though they were badly beaten, they refused to work as slaves. Meanwhile, Governor John Hancock of Massachusetts protested to the governor of Martinique, and the three men were returned to Boston. The affair drew an anguished petition to the Massachusetts legislature from a group of free blacks:

> The Petition of greet Number of Blacks freemen of this common welth Humbly sheweth that your Petitioners are justly Allarmed at the enhuman and cruel Treetment that Three of our Brethren free citizens of the Town of Boston lately Receved; The captain under a pertence that his vessel was in destres on an Island belo in this Hearber haven got them on bord put them in irons and carried them of, from their Wives & children to be sold for slaves.

The legislature responded to the free blacks' plea, passing a law forbidding the dragooning of free blacks into slavery. The law also gave blacks to whom that happened the right to recover damages from the kidnapper.

The supporters of slavery did not take all the antislavery activity lying down. They succeeded in getting two provisions favoring their cause into the U.S. Constitution, although on one of them they had to give some ground. They had originally sought to have slaves counted as part of the population, so that the slave states would get more representatives in Congress. Northern delegates to the constitutional convention resisted. The result was this wording in Article I, dealing with the House of Representatives: "Representatives . . . shall be apportioned among the several States . . . according to their respective Numbers [their population], which shall be determined by adding to the Whole Number of free Persons . . . three-fifths of all other persons." The "other persons" were the slaves. In other words, a slave counted as three-fifths of a person in determining how many congressmen a state would have.

The proslavery forces also got into Article IV a favorable provision on the treatment of fugitive slaves: "No Person held to Service or Labour in one State, under the Laws thereof, escaping into another, shall, in Consequence of any Law or Regulation therein, be discharged from such Service or Labour, but shall be delivered up on Claim of the Party to whom such Service or Labour may be due." That legalistic language meant that even if a slave escaped to a state having a law against slavery, he would have to be returned to his owner if the owner showed up and demanded to have his slave back. This provision, and the laws that rested on it, were to become a source of great friction between North and South in later years.

Before long, many states in the North had laws against slavery. Vermont had abolished it in 1777, during the Revolution. By 1804, the list of states prohibiting slavery included Massachusetts, New Hampshire, Rhode Island, Connecticut, Pennsylvania, New York and New Jersey. There never had been many slaves in the North, and most of the Northerners who owned slaves found the practice unprofitable. On farms in particular, slaves had to be supported all year whereas the growing season lasted only half the year.

As time went on, the chorus of voices in the North opposing slavery grew louder. Antislavery societies were established everywhere; in 1835 alone, 328 were formed, and by 1838 the American Anti-Slavery Society, the biggest and most prominent of the groups, could report the existence of some 1,350 societies having a total membership of 250,000 people. There were even some antislavery societies in the South until the climate there became so hostile that few Southerners dared to speak or act against slavery.

Added to the chorus was a large number of publications devoted to antislavery issues. Indeed, the first of them—the *Manumission Intelligencer*—appeared in the South, beginning in 1814.

Its publisher was Elihu Embree, founder also of a Southern anti-slavery society in Tennessee.

One should not conclude from all of this that the people in the North were unanimous against slavery or willing to consider blacks as the equals of whites. Many people in the North paid little or no attention to the slavery issue. Those who did—even most of the ardent abolitionists—could not see blacks as people to associate with except at arm's length. Free blacks in the North got mainly menial jobs such as porters and household servants. Whites avoided socializing with them. Many, perhaps most, saw blacks as inferior to whites, less intelligent and shiftless. The New York abolitionist Lewis Tappan confided in his diary how agonizing this attitude was to a white person who wanted to treat blacks as equals. "As Xians [Christians]—and xian abolitionists—will not tolerate my associating with my colored brethren in a white man's chh [church] it seems my duty to unite with a colored chh."

The story of Prudence Crandall shows how fierce the hostility of Northern whites to blacks could be. Miss Crandall was a young white woman who was described by people who knew her as attractive but not beautiful. She was also a Quaker who, like others of her religion, regarded slavery as a sin. In 1831, she opened a school for girls in the prosperous town of Canterbury, Connecticut: the Canterbury Female Boarding School. Things went well there for two years, but then Miss Crandall got an application from Sarah Harris, the daughter of a farmer. Sarah was black. Miss Crandall admitted her to the school, and the white townspeople were outraged. They withdrew their daughters from the school.

Miss Crandall, left with one pupil, decided to turn her institution into a school for "young Ladies and little Misses of color." With the help of several prominent abolitionists, she enrolled 20 girls from various parts of New England. That was too much for the white townspeople. They called a town meeting, at which they adopted a resolution declaring their opposition to "a school, for the people of color, at any place within the limits of this town." For some that was not enough; they jeered at the girls, broke windows in the school and set fires in the building. Turning to the state legislature, the town obtained a law making it illegal for anyone to open a school for students from out of the state without permission from the local authorities. Miss Crandall was arrested

The
just man shall
be in eternal
remembrance

Went to prison for
Teaching
Colored Children.

Prudence Crandall ran a school for girls in Connecticut. When she accepted a black girl as a pupil, the white parents withdrew their daughters. Miss Crandall turned the institution into a school for "young Ladies and little Misses of color." The townspeople persuaded the state to pass a law making such a school illegal. Miss Crandall was imprisoned for breaking the law. She eventually closed the school and moved away.

and jailed for violating this law. That made her a heroine for the abolitionists, but she gave up the school, married a Baptist minister and moved away.

The troubles of Sarah Harris and her family typified the problems of free blacks in the North. They were in the society but not really accepted by it. Freedom also worried slaveholders, because it was a goal that lured slaves and therefore represented a threat to slavery. In the view of many people, the best solution to the problem of free blacks was to send them back to Africa. This attitude led to the formation in 1817 of the American Colonization Society. In 1822, the society founded the colony of Liberia on the west coast of Africa as the place for resettling free blacks. By 1830, it had settled 1,430 people there.

But the idea never had much support among blacks, who resisted being uprooted. Peter Osborne, a prominent black in Connecticut, had this to say on the subject in 1832:

> What man would content himself, and say nothing of the rights of man, with two millions of his brethren in bondage? Let us contend for the prize. Let us all unite, and with one accord declare that we will not leave our own country to emigrate to Liberia, nor elsewhere, to be civilized nor christianized. Let us make known to America that we are not barbarians; that we are not inhuman beings; that this is our native country; that our forefathers have planted trees in America for us, and we intend to stay and eat the fruit. Our forefathers fought, bled and died to achieve the independence of the United States. Why should we forbear contending for the prize? It becomes every colored citizen in the United States to step forward boldly, and gallantly defend his rights.

Colonization also drew fire from Northern abolitionists because slaveholders supported it as a means of removing the temptation of freedom from the view of slaves, thereby strengthening the institution of slavery. Although colonization drew support as late as the Civil War, from a person as eminent as President Abraham Lincoln, the idea never achieved much success and gradually faded away.

Until about 1830, the argument over slavery was mainly a war of words. A 76-page pamphlet published in 1829, however, indicated that the bitterness was increasing on both sides. The author was David Walker, a free black who had moved in 1828 from North Carolina to Boston, where he set up as a dealer in second-hand clothes. His fiery words reflected the taste of the time for long titles: *Walker's Appeal in Four Articles Together with a Preamble to the Colored Citizens of the World, But in Particular and Very Expressly to those of the United States.* The pamphlet thundered against whites who held slaves or tolerated slavery and urged slaves to revolt against their bondage:

> *Are we men! . . . Did our creator make us to be slaves to dust and ashes like ourselves? . . . How could we be so submissive to a gang of men, whom we cannot tell whether they are as good as ourselves or not, I never conceive. . . . America is more our country than it is the whites—we have enriched it with our blood and tears. The greatest riches in all America have arisen from our blood and tears: And they will drive us from our property and homes, which we have earned with our blood.*

Walker's Appeal (the name that people usually gave it) was circulated widely in both the North and the South. It inflamed white Southerners, to the point where a group in Georgia offered a reward of $1,000 for anyone who would kill Walker and $10,000 if he were captured alive. (The idea of rewards for silencing opponents of slavery was new. In later years, similar rewards were offered for many white abolitionists.) Several Southern states responded to Walker's appeal by outlawing the education of blacks, who would therefore not be able to write or read inflammatory pamphlets, and by forbidding the circulation of such publications. It was evident that the whites of the South were ready to turn to harsher methods of defending slavery.

CHAPTER TWO NOTES

page 17   "No one can tell . . . " *Frederick Douglass,* **Life and Times of Frederick Douglass.** Boston: De Wolfe & Fiske Co., 1892, p. 608.

page 18   "O, ye nominal Christians! . . ." *Paul Edwards* (editor), **Equiano's Travels.** London: Heinemann, 1967, p. 32.

page 18   "what thing . . . " Quoted in *Francine Klagsbrun*, **Freedom Now!,** p. 9.

page 19   "He has waged . . . " Quoted in *Julian P. Boyd,* **The Declaration of Independence: Evolution of the Text.** Princeton: Princeton University Press, 1945, p. 20.

page 19   "tho' their people . . . " Quoted in *Julian P. Boyd,* **The Declaration of Independence: Evolution of the Text,** p. 37.

page 20   "The petition of greet Number . . . " Quoted in *Herbert Aptheker* (editor), **A Documentary History of the Negro People in the United States,** vol. 1, p. 20.

page 22   "As Xians . . . " Quoted in *Louis Filler,* **The Crusade Against Slavery,** p. 144.

page 22   "young Ladies . . . " **The Liberator,** Vol. III, No. 9, p. 35 (March 2, 1833).

page 24   "What man would content himself . . . " Quoted in *Herbert Aptheker* (editor), **A Documentary History of the Negro People in the United States,** vol. 1, p. 138.

page 25   "Are we men! . . . " Quoted in *John Hope Franklin,* **From Slavery to Freedom,** p. 243.

CHAPTER Three

THE SLAVEHOLDERS RESPOND

Arguments and Action

From the "twenty negers" of 1619, whose indentured servitude degenerated into slavery for their descendants, the number of black people working as slaves grew to more than two million by 1830. They had become crucial to the economy of the South, not only as a major source of labor but also as a form of property so valuable that Southern whites calculated their social standing on the basis of how many slaves they owned.

Looking back, it seems remarkable that an institution directly affecting only a small part of the population should have become so important in both the economy and the way of life of the South. By 1860, when slavery was at its peak, the number of families owning slaves in the South was (in round figures) 385,000 out of a population of 1,516,000 free families. Three out of four Southern whites had no direct connection with slavery. Moreover, most of the slaveholders worked small farms with fewer than 30 slaves. It was the owners of large plantations, holding at least 30 slaves and in some cases more than 100, who derived the most benefit from slavery and provided most of the clout for the defense of the institution. In 1860, this group numbered about 25,000 in a total slave-state population of 12,302,000—of which 8,098,000 were whites, 3,954,000 slaves and 250,000 free blacks.

Yet the whites who did not own slaves were as ardent as the slaveholders in defending the institution. They saw whites as a superior class, blacks as "inferior" people fitted only for slavery. Keeping the blacks in bondage meant that whites who held no slaves were spared black competition for jobs and social position and could regard themselves as members of a higher class.

As is so often the case when people set out to defend an institution that is basically indefensible, Southern whites advanced an array of arguments intended to show that slavery was a good thing, beneficial to both whites and blacks and crucial to the Southern economy. Fredrika Bremer, a Swedish woman who traveled extensively in the United States before the Civil War, said she had met few slaveholders who could "openly and honestly look the thing in the face." Instead, "They wind and turn about in all sorts of ways, and make use of every argument—sometimes the most opposite, to convince me that the slaves are the happiest people in the world, and do not wish to be placed in any other condition, or in any other relationship to their masters than that in which they find themselves." The 10 major arguments do not exhaust the list:

1. African people—the original indentured servants and their slave descendants—were barbarians who for their own good needed strict discipline and severe controls. Otherwise, the white civilization of the South would be endangered by the presence of these wild people.

2. Slavery would have a beneficial effect on blacks in the long run because it brought heathens from Africa into contact with Christianity, whose teachings would lead to the salvation of their souls. A. T. Bledsoe, a professor of mathematics at the University of Virginia who wrote extensively on the virtues of slavery, said: "No fact is plainer than that the blacks have been elevated and improved by their servitude in this country. We cannot possibly conceive, indeed, how Divine Providence could have placed them in a better school of correction."

3. The Bible supports slavery. This argument took many forms but relied heavily on the 25th chapter of Leviticus. As James Hammond put it, "God especially authorized his chosen people to purchase 'bondmen forever' from the heathen, as recorded in the twenty-fifth chapter of Leviticus. . . . " [That

The whip and the paddle were the primary means of disciplining slaves and controlling their behavior. James H. Hammond, who held a large number of slaves on his plantation in South Carolina, said that 100 lashes in a day would be an extreme punishment for a slave and that "in general, 15 to 20 lashes will be a sufficient flogging." This woodcut appeared in *The Suppressed Book About Slavery,* published in 1864.

passage says: "Both thy bondmen and thy bondmaids . . . shall be of the heathen. . . . "] Hammond also cited the Tenth Commandment ["Thou shalt not covet thy neighbor's . . . man-servant, nor his maid-servant. . . . "] and asked: "Does it not explicitly forbid you to disturb your neighbor in the enjoyment of his property?" (Remember that slaves were property.) William Harper, chancellor of South Carolina and also briefly a U.S. senator from that state, wrote: "*Servitude* is the condition of civilization. It was decreed, when the command was given, 'be fruitful, and multiply and replenish the earth, and subdue it,' and when it was added, 'in the sweat of thy face shalt thou eat bread.'" The South Carolina Court of Appeals spoke before the Civil War of "the solid moral and scriptural foundations upon which the institution of slavery rests."

4. Tradition supports slavery. Far from being an invention of the South, the institution went back to the dawn of civilization and was practiced by the ancient Greeks and Romans.

5. Only blacks were suited to work in the agricultural conditions of the South. Said *De Bow's Review* in 1856: "The

white man will never raise—can never raise—a cotton or a sugar crop in the United States. In our swamps and under our suns, the negro thrives but the white man dies." This view ignored the fact that white men had always done much of the South's heavy farm work.

6. Slavery was essential to the economy and prosperity of the South. James Hammond of South Carolina, the slaveholder who had so much to say about the value of the institution, put the matter this way: "In all social systems there must be a class to do the menial duties, to perform the drudgery of life. . . . Its requisites are vigor, docility, fidelity. Such a class you must have or you would not have that other class which leads progress, civilization, and refinement." (One would like to be able to ask Hammond how he thought the progress, civilization and refinement of Boston and other Northern cities came about.) On another occasion, addressing a letter to an abolitionist, he said: "Nay, supposing that we were all convinced, and thought of Slavery precisely as you do, at what era of 'moral suasion' do you imagine you could prevail on us to give up a thousand millions of dollars in the value of our slaves, and a thousand millions of dollars more in the depreciation of our lands, in consequence of the want of laborers to cultivate them?" John Milton, governor of Florida during the Civil War, wrote of the importance of agricultural labor to the South and to the Confederate war effort: "The advocates of Slavery; in our National Councils and throughout the various forms of arguments to sustain it, have contended forcibly and truthfully, that negroes had not the inclination or ability to labor successfully, without the superior skill of the White man to direct and enforce their labor."

7. Blacks as a race had certain traits that made them particularly suitable for slavery. The *Jackson Mississippian* said in 1856 that "nature's God intended the African for the status of slavery." Most white Americans, in the North as well as the South, thought that blacks were naturally savage, lazy and childlike and so could not be taken into white society as equals. The former slave Frederick Douglass had an answer to these views: "Take any race you please, French, English, Irish, or Scotch, subject them to slavery for ages—regard them and treat them every where, every way, as property. . . . Let them be loaded with chains, scarred with the whip, branded with hot irons, sold in the market, kept in ignorance . . . and I venture to say that the same doubt would spring up concerning either of them, which now confronts the negro."

One of the most agonizing ordeals slaves had to endure was the "selling away" of family members, who frequently were never heard from again. Harriet Beecher Stowe describes such a scene in her influential antislavery novel *Uncle Tom's Cabin,* for which this drawing was made by George Cruikshank.

8. Owners and slaves lived comfortably together in the South, as reflected in a statistic revealed by a census of the insane done by the United States as part of the census of 1840. It showed that one of every 1,558 blacks in the slave states was insane or idiotic, compared with one in every 144.5 in the free states. To put it another way, the rate of mental disturbance was about 11 times higher among free blacks than among slaves.

Southern whites made much of this finding. John C. Calhoun, a prominent defender of slavery who at the time of the census was a United States senator from South Carolina, said: "Here is proof of the necessity of slavery. The African is incapable of self-care and sinks into lunacy under the burden of freedom. It is a mercy to him to give him the guardianship and protection from mental death." Slavery had now become good for the slaves.

What the census did not show was that few mental institutions in the South admitted blacks. Moreover, the slaveholder had strong economic reasons to keep his mentally disturbed slaves out of mental institutions. He had to pay to keep them there (if he could find a mental institution to admit them), and meanwhile he lost their labor. So he tolerated a good deal of strange mental behavior, calling it "eccentricity" rather than reporting it as insanity.

9. Slavery enhanced the social and economic position of whites. This was such a self-serving argument that it was not often spoken aloud, but it lay close to the heart of the South's defense of its peculiar institution. The argument did surface in a Georgia newspaper, the *Columbus Times,* in 1856: "It is African slavery that makes every white man in a sense a lord—it draws a broad distinction between the two races, and color gives caste. . . . Here the distinction is between white free men and black slaves, and every white is, and feels that he is, a MAN." Chancellor Harper said: "It is by the existence of Slavery, exempting so large a portion of our citizens from the necessity of bodily labor, that we have a greater proportion than any other people, who have leisure for intellectual pursuits. . . . "

10. Blacks were an inferior race, fitted only to occupy low positions. George S. Sawyer, in his *Southern Institutes,* wrote: "The social, moral, and political, as well as the physical history of the negro race bears strong testimony against them; it furnishes the most undeniable proof of their mental inferiority. In no age or condition has the real negro shown a capacity to throw off the chains of barbarism and brutality that have bound down the nations of that race; or to rise above the common cloud of darkness that still broods over them." Samuel A. Cartwright, a physician in New Orleans, found several racial traits that demonstrated the black's inferiority. One was: "The Melanic [black] race have a much stronger propensity to indulge in the intemperate use of ardent spirits than white people." A second was: "That negroes consume less oxygen than the white race, is proved by their motions being proverbially much slower, and their want of muscular and mental activity." A third was that the black is "anatomically constructed, about the head and face, more like the monkey tribes and the lower order of animals than any other species of the genus man."

Whatever force these arguments had among Southern whites, it was evident in many ways that the slaves did not look on slavery as an enjoyable condition. From the beginning, there was a steady flow of slaves attempting to escape to freedom. As early as 1793, Southerners moved to deal with this problem by persuading Congress to enact the first of several laws bearing the name of Fugitive Slave Act. All of them were intended to put teeth into the provision of the Constitution that a slave remained the property of his owner even if he escaped to a free state. The first law said that the master of a slave who had done that could recapture the slave, take him before the nearest federal or state judge and obtain an order for the return of the slave to the master's property. The slave was not allowed a trial by a jury; it took only the master's word to put him back in bondage.

Slaves also showed their hatred of slavery by numerous revolts, some small and some large. About 250 slave uprisings are known to have taken place in the 200 years before the Civil War; there were probably many more. A revolt in Virginia led by Gabriel, owned by a man named Prosser and therefore known as Gabriel Prosser, came closer to success than most and also showed the depth of the fear that Southern whites had of slave revolts.

Gabriel, aided by his wife Nanny and his brothers Solomon and Martin, quietly lined up a substantial number of slaves behind a plan to attack Richmond, intending to capture the large stores of weapons there and then to expand the revolt. Gabriel's recruits spent much of their time making their own crude weapons. By late August of 1800 the group had assembled for the attack. But on August 30, the day chosen for the attack, a heavy storm flooded roads and washed out bridges, preventing the attackers from moving. Meanwhile, two slaves revealed Gabriel's plan to their owner, and he told the governor—James Monroe, future president of the United States (1817–1825). Monroe called out the militia. Between the weather and the troops, Gabriel's group was forced to disband. Gabriel and some 35 other participants were hanged.

Gabriel's revolt, like virtually every effort by blacks to seek freedom, caused Southern whites to be harsher in their treatment of slaves and impelled Southern states to tighten the "black codes" that regulated the behavior of slaves. The codes even regulated the behavior of whites to some extent—as in forbidding them to teach blacks to read or write, on penalty of fines and jail terms.

The fears of Southern whites extended also to free blacks, who were seen as likely to inspire slaves to seek their own freedom. South Carolina imprisoned free blacks serving as seamen on foreign ships stopping at ports in the state and made the seamen pay the cost of the imprisonment. Those who failed to pay were sold as slaves. More than 40 ships lost crewmen in this way. Mississippi made each free black post a bond of $100 to ensure that he would not cause trouble; those who failed were sold as slaves.

As the white people of the South grew fiercer in their defense of slavery and harsher in their treatment of blacks, an increasing number of people in the North turned to the view that slavery was evil and should be abolished. The stage was set for two events of 1831 that escalated the hard words on both sides, leading to a series of bitter confrontations that culminated in the Civil War.

CHAPTER THREE NOTES

page 28   "openly and honestly . . ." *Fredrika Bremer,* **The Homes of the New World.** New York: Harper & Brothers, 1854, vol. 1, p. 282.

page 28   "No fact is plainer . . ." *E. N. Elliott* (editor), **Cotton Is King.** New York: Johnson Reprint Corp., 1968, p. 416.

page 28   "God especially . . . " **The Pro-Slavery Argument,** p. 106.

page 29   "Does it not . . . " **The Pro-Slavery Argument,** p. 105.

page 29   *Servitude* is . . . " **The Pro-Slavery Argument,** p. 27.

page 29   "the solid moral . . . " Quoted in *Kenneth M. Stampp,* **The Peculiar Institution,** p. 234.

page 29   "The white man . . . " Quoted in *Kenneth M. Stampp,* **The Peculiar Institution,** p. 7.

page 30   "In all social systems . . . " Quoted in *John Hope Franklin,* **From Slavery to Freedom,** p. 262.

page 30   "Nay, supposing . . . " **The Pro-Slavery Argument,** p. 141.

page 30   "The advocates of Slavery . . . " Quoted in *Ira Berlin,* et al. (editors), **Free at Last,** p. 130.

page 30   "nature's God . . . " Quoted in *Kenneth M. Stampp,* **The Peculiar Institution,** p. 215.

page 30   "Take any race . . . " Quoted in *James M. McPherson,* **The Struggle for Equality,** p. 149.

page 31   "Here is proof . . . " Quoted in *Albert Deutsch,* **Bulletin of the History of Medicine.** Baltimore: Johns Hopkins University Press, vol. XV #5, May 1944, p. 473.

page 32   "It is African slavery . . . " Quoted in *Kenneth M. Stampp,* **The Peculiar Institution,** pp. 425–426.

page 32   "It is by the existence . . . " **The Pro-Slavery Argument,** p. 35.

page 32   "The social, moral, and political . . . " Quoted in *John Hope Franklin,* **From Slavery to Freedom,** p. 262.

page 32   "The Melanic race . . . " *E. N. Elliott* (editor), **Cotton Is King,** p. 694.

page 32   "That negroes consume . . . " *E. N. Elliott* (editor), **Cotton Is King,** p. 698.

page 32   "anatomically constructed . . . " *E. N. Elliott* (editor), **Cotton Is King,** p. 707.

CHAPTER Four

THE BATTLE JOINED
Violence Short of War

Two men, one black and one white, did much to stoke the fires of the argument over slavery. The black was Nat Turner, who for most of his short life in Southampton County, Virginia, had seemed to be what an owner would call a good slave—obedient, deferential and attentive to his work for Joseph Travis, his master. He did run away once, but he soon returned. In his spare time he was a preacher. At some point he came to believe that he had been chosen by God to lead his people out of slavery. He persuaded a few other slaves to join him. In February of 1831, he took a solar eclipse as a sign from God, and he accordingly set July 4, 1831—Independence Day—as the time to strike. But Turner was sick that day, and so he waited for another sign, which came to him in August in the form of a blue cast to the sun. He called for the revolt to begin on August 21. On that day, Turner and his small band killed Travis and the rest of the Travis family and began to march on Jerusalem, the county seat. Other slaves joined the group on the way, bringing the number of marchers to about 70. Within 24 hours they had killed some 60 white people. But the alarm had been sounded. State and federal troops intercepted the blacks and killed most of them, along with scores of other slaves who had not taken part in the revolt. Turner escaped and hid for several weeks in a cave. Hunted relentlessly, he was captured on October 30 and hanged on November 11.

The impact on the South of Turner's revolt was profound. Slave rebellion was what Southern whites feared most, and it had happened in Southampton County. Several states called emergency sessions of their legislature, which responded by making the black codes even harsher. Among other things, because Turner had been a preacher, the stiffened codes forbade both slaves and free blacks to preach or to hold religious services.

The other catalyst in the debate over slavery was William Lloyd Garrison. Peering at the world through oval spectacles of the type common at the time, he looked mild, and indeed he was said to be good natured in private. In public he was a ferocious and uncompromising champion of many causes: for temperance and women's rights, against tobacco, theaters and capital punishment—and, above all, slavery. One might imagine him as a fire-and-brimstone preacher, but in fact he was a printer and publisher and a tireless public speaker. (Not a very good speaker, according to his fellow abolitionist Thomas Wentworth Higginson, who described Garrison's speeches as "usually monotonous, sometimes fatiguing, but always controlling.")

As a young man, Garrison wrote for and edited several newspapers, his words on the abolition of slavery gradually becoming stronger. On January 1, 1831, he published in Boston the first issue of his newspaper, *The Liberator*, which quickly became the leading voice of the abolitionist movement. In the first issue, he said he would persist "till every chain be broken, and every bondsman set free!" And he made clear what his tone would be:

> I will be as harsh as truth, and as uncompromising as
> justice. On this subject, I do not wish to think, or speak,
> or write, with moderation. No! No! Tell a man, whose
> house is on fire, to give a moderate alarm; tell him to
> moderately rescue his wife from the hands of the
> ravisher; tell the mother to gradually extricate her babe
> from the fire into which it has fallen; but urge me not to
> use moderation in a cause like the present. I am in
> earnest—I will not equivocate—I will not excuse—I will
> not retreat a single inch—AND I WILL BE HEARD.

Heard he was, particularly in the South. *The Liberator* never had a very large circulation, being bought chiefly by abolitionists in the North, but it struck a nerve among white Southerners. They saw its strong words and its regular accounts of the cruelties of slavery as evidence that antislavery sentiment was becoming passionate in the North. ("The truth is," the historian Gilbert H.

William Lloyd Garrison, publisher of *The Liberator,* was about 60 years old at the time of this photograph. A mild and courteous man at home, he was ferocious in his public campaigns for temperance and women's rights and against tobacco, the theater and—above all—slavery.

Barnes wrote in 1933, "that the *Liberator* was made famous not by its Northern supporters but by its Southern enemies.")

Garrison made enemies in the South by sending copies of *The Liberator* to Southern newspaper editors. They were so alarmed by his attacks on slavery that they responded with heated attacks on him in their papers. Garrison would then reprint in *The Liberator* his original article together with the Southern responses, thus fueling the growing conflict between North and South over slavery.

Some of his Southern enemies were so goaded by Garrison that they put a price on his head and tried to prevent the distribution of his newspaper. Only nine months after *The Liberator* began publication, the Georgia legislature offered a reward of $4,000 for Garrison's arrest. A vigilance committee in South Carolina said it would pay $1,500 for the arrest of anyone who distributed *The Liberator*. To be known as a reader of the paper brought the risk of punishment in the South. A man in Georgia who subscribed to the paper was pulled from his home by a mob, tarred and feathered and tied to a post for a whipping.

Garrison's fierce voice led a growing chorus of Northerners calling for the abolition of slavery. Benjamin Lundy, a Quaker, became an abolitionist when he saw slaves in Wheeling, Virginia (now West Virginia), chained together on their way to a slave market. He formed in Ohio one of the first antislavery societies and began publishing in Baltimore one of the first antislavery papers, the *Genius of Universal Emancipation*. Garrison worked there with Lundy for a time. One of the editorials he wrote attacked Francis Todd, a merchant in Massachusetts, for participating in the domestic slave trade. Todd sued for libel. A jury found Garrison guilty and fined him $50 plus costs, the total coming to about $100. Because Garrison could not pay, he was sent to jail. Before his term ended, a wealthy businessman from New York paid the fine and Garrison was released.

The wealthy businessman was Arthur Tappan, who with his brother Lewis contributed much time and money to the antislavery movement. They and Garrison were among the leaders in the founding of the American Anti-Slavery Society in 1833, a move that solidified the abolitionist movement in the North. Its constitution made plain what the founders sought:

THE LIBERATOR.

VOL. I.]   WILLIAM LLOYD GARRISON AND ISAAC KNAPP, PUBLISHERS.   [NO. 33.

BOSTON, MASSACHUSETTS.]   OUR COUNTRY IS THE WORLD—OUR COUNTRYMEN ARE MANKIND.   [SATURDAY, AUGUST 13, 1831.

One of the most influential antislavery publications was *The Liberator,* a weekly newspaper issued by William Lloyd Garrison from 1831 to the end of 1865, when the slaves had been freed as a result of the Civil War. Note the sign on the auctioneer's desk in the picture above the title.

The object of this Society is the entire abolition of slavery in the United States. . . . It [the society] shall aim to convince all our fellow-citizens, by arguments addressed to their understandings and consciences, that slave-holding is a heinous crime in the sight of God, and that the duty, safety, and best interests of all concerned, requires its immediate abandonment.

Gradually, Garrison and the movement broadened their support among prominent people. Samuel J. May, a Unitarian minister in Connecticut, heard an antislavery speech Garrison made in 1830 while he was on a lecture tour to raise money for starting *The Liberator.* May's reaction was: "That is a providential man! He is a prophet; he will shake our nation to its center, but he will shake slavery out of it."

Theodore D. Weld, a transplanted New Englander, had a leading role in setting up two centers of abolitionist activity in the West. The first was Lane Seminary in Cincinnati. There, in 1834, Weld organized the Lane Debate on slavery, which went on for nine days and ended with a strong "yes" vote on the question. "Ought the people of the slave-holding states to abolish slavery immediately?" That was too much for Lane's conservative board of trustees, which broke up the antislavery society that had been formed by some radical students. Weld and 40 students resigned from the seminary and transferred to the Oberlin Institute in Ohio.

When Weld and his followers persuaded the institute to take an antislavery position and admit blacks, Arthur Tappan provided the money that put the struggling institute on its feet as Oberlin College. There Weld trained some 70 students to be agents for the American Anti-Slavery Society, carrying the antislavery argument ardently to many parts of the country.

In 1839, Weld published a book that further cemented the hard feelings between North and South. *American Slavery As It Is: Testimony of a Thousand Witnesses* presented accounts of the cruel treatment of slaves that Weld and his wife, Angelina, and his sister-in-law, Sarah Grimké, had culled from Southern newspapers and other sources. One of their entries, drawn from the *North Carolina Standard* of July 18, 1838, read in part: "TWENTY DOLLARS REWARD. Ranaway from the subscriber [the signer of the notice, Micajah Ricks], a negro woman & two children; the woman is tall & black, and a few days before she went off, I burnt her with a hot iron on the left side of her face; I tried to make the letter M. . . . " The book sold well and soon became a source of antislavery arguments for abolitionist lecturers.

The Grimké sisters, Angelina and Sarah, were unusual among abolitionists because they came from the South—South Carolina, where their father owned a plantation and many slaves. Even as girls, they were uneasy about slavery. Sarah wrote later that she had taught her maid to read and write in defiance of the state's laws forbidding whites to do that for slaves. "I took an almost malicious satisfaction in teaching my little waiting-maid at night, when she was supposed to be occupied in combing and brushing my long locks. The light was put out, the keyhole screened, and flat on our stomachs, before the fire, we defied the laws of South Carolina."

Sarah Grimké, 13 years older than Angelina, broke away from the South first, moving to Philadelphia and becoming a Quaker. Angelina, already a Quaker, followed her there in 1829. Both became eloquent and popular antislavery speakers, made the more effective because of their firsthand knowledge of slavery. "I stand before you as a Southerner," Angelina said in a typical speech, "exiled from the land of my birth by the sound of the lash and the piteous cry of the slave. I stand before you as a moral being and as a moral being I feel that I owe it to the suffering slave and to the deluded master, to my country and to the world to do all that I can to overturn a system of complicated crimes. . . . "

Another Southerner who turned against slavery was James G. Birney, once a slaveholder in Kentucky. He freed his slaves in 1834 and joined the American Anti-Slavery Society, of which he soon

Theodore D. Weld was a prominent abolitionist who, with his wife, published *American Slavery As It Is: Testimony of a Thousand Witnesses* in 1839. Its tales of cruelty to slaves had a strong influence on the abolitionist movement. Weld's wife was Angelina Grimké, a woman born to a slave-owning family in South Carolina. She and her sister Sarah Grimké were influential proponents of abolition.

became vice president. In 1836 he founded an antislavery newspaper, the *Philanthropist*. In 1840 his supporters, believing their views against slavery to be getting little attention from the major political parties, founded the Liberty Party and nominated Birney for president. He received about 4,000 votes. Four years later, the party nominated him again; this time he got some 62,000 votes—a respectable showing for a minority party.

The abolitionists also had on their side the powerful voices of the poets John Greenleaf Whittier and James Russell Lowell. Both wrote thundering antislavery poems. In addition, Whittier published in 1833 a pamphlet *Justice and Expediency*, that was widely circulated with financial help from Arthur Tappan and became a major abolitionist paper. Lowell wrote for the *Anti-Slavery Standard*.

Particularly effective in speaking and acting against slavery, and particularly irritating to white Southerners, were several free blacks who could tell from personal experience what it was like to be a slave. The most prominent among them was Frederick Douglass, who had escaped to freedom in 1838, four years after his year of misery with the "slave-breaker" Edward Covey. He was at an antislavery meeting in Massachusetts in 1841 when he was asked unexpectedly to speak. His story—he was naturally well spoken and in time developed a commanding public presence—profoundly moved his audience. It was the first of many audiences to hear and be moved by his arguments against slavery. In 1845, he published the story as a book, *Narrative of the Life of Frederick Douglass, an American Slave*, which quickly became a best-seller. Douglass used to say, when people asked him where he got his education, "Massachusetts Abolition University: Mr. Garrison, president."

Another free black who spoke movingly against slavery was the woman who took the name Sojourner Truth. Under the name of Isabella Van Wagener, she had been a slave in New York before that state abolished slavery. Her tales of that life, delivered with fervor in a deep voice, made a powerful impression on Northern audiences. She called herself Sojourner to describe her life of wandering from place to place and Truth because, she said, God is Truth and she saw herself as a messenger of God. Her life story,

Narrative of Sojourner Truth, a Northern Slave, was published in 1850.

The shots the abolitionists fired against the South and its peculiar institution pounded away at the idea that slavery was evil and unjustifiable. Slavery defied the teachings of Christianity, which held that God created all men in His own image and that Jesus had preached the brotherhood of man. It caused inhumane treatment of one group of humans by another. It brought out the

Frederick Douglass was probably the most articulate and influential escaped slave. He was a powerful speaker and a moving writer about his experiences as a slave, and his words contributed strongly to the abolitionist movement.

worst in Southern whites, whether they owned slaves or not. But the fundamental argument of the abolitionists was that slavery violated the clear statement in the Declaration of Independence that "all Men are created equal, that they are endowed by their Creator with certain unalienable Rights, that among these are Life, Liberty, and the Pursuit of Happiness."

To whites in the South, the abolitionists were nothing but trouble. Southern states passed laws forbidding the establishment of antislavery groups in their territory. Southern whites who spoke out against slavery, such as Birney and the Grimké sisters, were made to feel so uncomfortable if not unsafe that they left the South or fell silent. People in the South made strenuous and sometimes violent efforts to keep abolitionist lecturers, newspapers and pamphlets out of the South.

A typical effort took place in Charleston, South Carolina, in July of 1835, when a group of whites broke into the post office, seized antislavery newspapers and pamphlets and burned them in the public square. The Charleston postmaster did nothing about this attack and in fact indicated that he approved of it. Abolitionists took the case to the U.S. postmaster general, Amos Kendall, who supported the Charleston postmaster. So did the president, Andrew Jackson, himself a Southerner and a slaveholder. He declared that abolitionist publications were a "wicked plan of inciting Negroes to insurrection and massacre." He even asked Congress to pass a law to "prohibit . . . the circulation in the Southern states, through the mail, of incendiary publications intended to instigate the slaves to insurrection." The law did not pass, having been defeated in the Senate on a close vote. Indeed, the abolitionists emerged with a victory. So many people outside the South expressed outrage at the disclosures of interference with the mails that Congress was moved to pass a law requiring postal officials to deliver all the mail that came into their hands.

One could take it for granted that abolitionists would be opposed in the South, but they were not universally popular in the North, either. Many Northerners did business in the South and feared that abolitionist activity would harm their business. Garrison came within an inch of his life in an attack by such a group. He and the British abolitionist George Thompson were scheduled to speak at a meeting of the Boston Female Anti-Slavery Society on October 21, 1835. An anonymous handbill distributed shortly after noon that day urged "friends of the Union" to *"snake Thompson out!"* and announced that "A purse of $100 has been raised by a number of patriotic citizens to reward the individual who shall first lay violent hands on Thompson, so that he may be brought to the tarkettle before dark." The handbill drew about 200 protesting people, mostly well-dressed businessmen, to the meeting place. Thompson did not appear. When Garrison tried to leave, the mob seized him and put a rope around his neck. He was rescued by two men who led him through the crowd to safety in City Hall. A member of the group told him later that the plan had been "to take you and Mr. Thompson to the Common, strip, tar-and-feather you, and then dye your face and hands black in a manner that would never change from a night negro color."

A worse fate awaited Elijah Lovejoy, who published an anti-slavery newspaper, the *Observer,* in Alton, Illinois. Being a port town on the Mississippi River near St. Louis, Alton did business with both North and South. Three times in 1836 and 1837 anti-abolitionist mobs destroyed Lovejoy's press. Supporters helped him get new ones. The fourth press was due to arrive on November 7, 1837, and Lovejoy's supporters made plans to help him defend it. Late that night, a mob attacked and set fire to the warehouse where the press was stored. Lovejoy, trying to put out the fire, was shot and killed. He thus became a martyr to the abolitionist movement and to the principle of a free press.

Lovejoy's murder, said former president John Quincy Adams, caused "a shock as of an earthquake throughout this continent." Meetings to honor Lovejoy and to protest the manner of his death were held all over the country. It was evident from the murder and the reaction to it that the battle over slavery was turning toward violence.

Fugitive slaves were a constant source of friction between North and South. Slave owners in the South felt that they had every right under the law—the Fugitive Slave Act of 1793 and similarly named acts passed later to clarify or tighten up the laws—to go North and reclaim slaves who had escaped to freedom. Northern sentiment lay with the fugitives, recognizing that each of them had gone through an ordeal to escape from bondage. People in the North were outraged by the zeal of slave owners in recapturing fugitives and by the fact that blacks who had become legally free were often seized in the North and sent into slavery.

In an effort to help fugitives and prevent the seizure of free blacks, Pennsylvania passed in 1826 a law giving the state's courts the power to rule on disputes arising under the Fugitive Slave Act. In other words, a Southern slave owner would have to take his case into a Northern court before he could reclaim a fugitive slave. It was not a promising situation for a slave owner.

A challenge to this law in the U.S. Supreme Court produced a decision *(Prigg v. Pennsylvania)* in 1842 that seemed to favor the Southern position. The decision said states could not pass laws on fugitive slaves because Congress had made that a federal matter. But Justice Joseph Story added a comment expressing doubt that state officials could be made to enforce the federal law.

Northern states were quick to seize this opening. They began passing "personal-liberty laws" that made it difficult for federal officials to enforce the law and easy for state officials to frustrate slave catchers. Southerners responded by demanding tighter provisions in the federal laws. This issue became tangled in the argument over whether slavery should be allowed in territories acquired as a result of the Mexican War. As a gesture to the South, Congress included in the Compromise of 1850 a provision intended to set up federal machinery for enforcing the fugitive slave laws. This provision did little to improve the success of slave catchers in the North, but it drew strong opposition there and strengthened support for the abolitionists.

Another cause of hard feeling and occasional violence was the prolonged battle over whether states joining the rapidly expanding nation should be slave or free states. As of 1818, the lineup of states for and against slavery already in the Union was equal—11 free, 11 slave. The question then was what to do about Missouri, which had applied for admission as the 23rd state with a constitution that permitted slavery. Northerners argued that Congress should not grant statehood to Missouri without prohibiting slavery there. Southerners insisted that Congress did not have the power to impose such a restriction on a new state. The solution this time was to have what is now Maine split off from Massachusetts and apply for admission at the same time. Under the Missouri Compromise of 1820, Missouri and Maine were made states without reference to slavery. The effect was to keep the lineup of slave and free states even. But the law also declared that in the remainder of the Louisiana Territory (of which Missouri had been part) north of Missouri's southern boundary, "slavery and involuntary servitude . . . shall be and is hereby forever prohibited."

The issue was bound to come up again, and it did after the United States acquired large territories from Mexico as a result of the Mexican War (1846–1848). Texas had already fought for and won independence from Mexico in 1836 and had joined the United States as a slave state in 1845. California, acquired in the Mexican War, soon applied for statehood. The U.S. House of Representatives wanted to prohibit slavery in all the territories taken from Mexico and said so twice (in 1846 and 1847) in the Wilmot Proviso, sponsored by Representative David Wilmot, an antislavery Democrat from Pennsylvania. The Senate would not accept the proviso. Another compromise had to be worked out. The Compromise of 1850 admitted California as a free state but allowed the rest of the Mexican territories to be organized without any advance prohibition of slavery.

The battle over slavery in Kansas showed how heated the issue could become. Congress in 1854 adopted the Kansas-Nebraska Act to admit Kansas and Nebraska as states. The law said that each of the states could settle the slavery issue for itself. Nebraska clearly would be a free state. The expectation was that Kansas, being geographically associated with the slave states, would become a slave state.

This prospect alarmed many people in the North. In Massachusetts, Eli Thayer and others formed what they called the Emigrant Aid Company to encourage Northern and presumably antislavery people to move to Kansas. The first group sent out by the company arrived there in August of 1854 and settled at the site that was to become Lawrence. Extensive advertising by the Emigrant Aid Company, together with a widespread interest among people of the East in taking advantage of the economic opportunities in the West, resulted in a large number of free-state supporters settling in Kansas.

Meanwhile, a large group in the neighboring slave state of Missouri was taking steps to make sure that Kansas would come in as a slave state. On March 30, 1855, when Kansans were voting on the membership of the territorial legislature that would decide the slavery question, some 5,000 armed men from Missouri entered Kansas and made sure that the vote resulted in a proslavery victory. The legislature thus chosen adopted a proslavery constitution. In October the free-state supporters drafted a constitution prohibiting slavery. On May 21, 1856, a proslavery mob sacked Lawrence. For several months thereafter, Kansas was in what amounted to a state of war over the slavery issue. "Bleeding Kansas," the newspapers of the North dubbed the turmoil. The newly organized Republican Party adopted "Bleeding Kansas" as a slogan in the presidential campaign of 1856, making slavery and the violent activities of the proslavery forces a major issue of the campaign. But slavery was not yet the dominant issue concerning voters in the election, and the Republicans lost to a proslavery Democratic ticket led by James Buchanan.

In 1857, after more maneuvering, the territorial legislature put a proslavery constitution before the voters of Kansas. The free-state supporters refused to participate in the vote, so the proslavery constitution won. President James Buchanan sent that constitution as part of Kansas's petition for statehood to Congress for a vote. The Senate approved a bill admitting Kansas as a state with the proslavery constitution. The House of Representatives attached a provision, which the Senate accepted, that the people of Kansas be given another chance to vote on the constitution. In August 1858, voting with little or no interference, the people of Kansas rejected the proslavery constitution. Kansas entered the Union as a free state in January 1861. That was a month after South Carolina had become the first state to secede—to declare that it was leaving the Union because of what it saw as interference with slavery. The issue of slavery was about to be decided by war.

Whatever the state of the fugitive slave laws and their enforcement, the flow of slaves escaping to freedom continued unabated. It was greatly aided by a network of whites and blacks in the North that came to be known as the Underground Railroad. How that name arose is a bit of a mystery. Among the explanations is one that sounds plausible. It involves Tice Davids, a slave who escaped from his master in Kentucky and made his way safely to freedom in Ohio. The master had pursued Davids closely but lost track of him after he swam across the Ohio River. The owner got across the river by boat soon afterward but could find no trace of his slave and no one who would admit having seen the fugitive. Baffled by the slave's disappearance, the master declared that Davids must have "gone off on an underground railroad."

The system was underground in the sense that it operated secretly, out of view of the law and of slave catchers. It was a railroad in the sense that it had a series of "stations" where people sheltered fugitive slaves and helped them on their way to the next station.

It is hard now to grasp what a risky undertaking it was for a slave to try to escape, particularly while he was still in slave territory. Any black person out on the roads was likely to be stopped by a white person and asked to show a pass stating that he was free or had permission to be away from his owner. Escaping slaves had to travel at night, often in disguise. Much or all of the journey had to be on foot, meaning that the fugitive could carry little in the way of food and possessions.

The story of a young couple who gained protection from the Underground Railroad in Philadelphia was related by William Wells Brown, himself an escaped slave who had become an abolitionist. His account appeared in *The Liberator* early in 1849:

> One of the most interesting cases of the escape of
> fugitives from American slavery that have ever come
> before the American people, has just occurred, under the
> following circumstances:—William and Ellen Craft, man
> and wife, lived with different masters in the State of
> Georgia. Ellen is so near white, that she can pass without
> suspicion for a white woman. Her husband is much
> darker. He is a mechanic, and by working nights and
> Sundays, he laid up money enough to bring himself and
> his wife out of slavery. Their plan was without precedent;
> and though novel, was the means of getting them their
> freedom. Ellen dressed in man's clothing, and passed as
> the master, while her husband passed as the servant. In
> this way they traveled from Georgia to Philadelphia.
> They are now out of reach of the blood-hounds of the

South. On their journey, they put up at the best hotels where they stopped. Neither of them can read or write. And Ellen, knowing that she would be called upon to write her name at the hotels, &c, tied her right hand up as though it was lame, which proved of some service to her, as she was called upon several times at hotels to "register" her name. In Charleston, S.C., they put up at the hotel where Gov. M'Duffie and John C. Calhoun generally make their home, yet these distinguished advocates of the "peculiar institution" say that the slaves cannot take care of themselves. They arrived in Philadelphia, in four days from the time they started. . . . They are now hid away within 25 miles of Philadelphia.

An escaping slave was lucky if he could have help from someone who had been through the experience. One such helper became famous for her success. She was Harriet Tubman, a small woman who escaped from slavery in Maryland in 1849 and made it safely to Philadelphia. From there she made repeated trips back into slave territory to lead groups of slaves to stations on the Underground Railroad. Nineteen times at least she undertook this hazardous task, bringing some 300 slaves to freedom.

Because of the secrecy of the Underground Railroad's operations, it is impossible to say how many "passengers" it carried to freedom. Estimates range as high as 50,000 in the 30 years preceding the Civil War. Out of four million slaves, that is a small number. But the very idea of the Underground Railroad—that whites and free blacks were helping slaves to escape—infuriated Southern whites, as the tales of slavery told by the fugitives increased abolitionist sentiment in the North. The railroad's activities heightened the tension between South and North over slavery.

The tension increased considerably in 1851 when Harriet Beecher Stowe, who had operated a station on the Underground Railroad, published her novel, *Uncle Tom's Cabin*, first in weekly installments (1851–1852) in *The National Era*, an antislavery weekly newspaper published in Washington by Gamaliel Bailey, and then (1852) as a book. A book could have a tremendous impact in those days before radio, television and motion pictures, and this one did. It told the story of Uncle Tom, a loyal and religious slave

Harriet Tubman was an escaped slave who, after gaining her freedom in the North, made many trips back into the South to help other slaves escape. She made at least 19 such trips, bringing some 300 slaves to freedom.

whose kindly owner, George Shelby, has to sell him for financial reasons. Shelby promises that he will reclaim Tom when he can. Tom, separated from his wife and children, eventually winds up as the property of Simon Legree, a cruel and uncouth planter. A time comes when Legree believes Tom knows where two missing female slaves can be found. Tom refuses to tell, and Legree has him flogged to the point of death. As Tom is dying, Shelby appears and is profoundly shocked by the scene. He sees to Tom's burial and, kneeling on the grave, says, "from this hour, I will do *what one man can* to drive out this curse of slavery from my land!"

The book's impact came from its vivid details about the cruelties visited on slaves and the bleakness of slave life. As far as is known, Mrs. Stowe visited slave territory only once, on a trip to Kentucky. But as a young woman she lived in Cincinnati, a city that saw a steady stream of fugitive slaves escaping over the Ohio River from Kentucky. From them she heard a great deal about slave life, and her reading and imagination supplied the additional details she put in the book.

Uncle Tom's Cabin sold more than 300,000 copies in the first year after it was published. Many plays were based on the book, increasing its influence. The tale had struck a nerve among people in the North who wanted to know more of what they had been hearing about the evils of slavery. What they read brought many of them to the side of the abolitionists. In the South, the book was reviled, and being found with a copy soon meant trouble for the seller, buyer or reader. As Philip Van Doren Stern put it in an annotated version of Mrs. Stowe's novel that he published in 1964: "This was the book which first brought the problem of Negro slavery in America to the attention of the entire world. . . . *Uncle Tom's Cabin* struck the world with explosive force. Its timing was just right, and it became not merely one of the greatest bestsellers in history, but a social document which influenced public opinion everywhere—even, in fact, the South, where it had a clandestine circulation because its sale was forbidden there."

Two other writers who are less remembered now also made strong contributions to the antislavery cause. One was Frederick Law Olmstead, later famous as the designer of Central Park in New York. In 1852 he began a series of journeys through the South that resulted in a series of books reporting what he had seen. In them he concluded that slavery was bringing the South to financial ruin by stifling the advance of new techniques in agriculture, by making the region remain agricultural instead of developing industries and by taking up large numbers of jobs that could have been held by paid workers. The other writer was Hinton Rowan Helper, a Southerner by birth, who made a similar argument in *The Impending Crisis,* published in 1857. "Within its [slavery's] pestilential atmosphere," he wrote, "nothing succeeds; progress and prosperity are unknown; inanition and slothfulness ensue." Both books attracted much attention in the North and caused alarm in the South.

It was inevitable that an issue so bitterly argued between abolitionists in the North and whites in the South would eventually reach the political battlefield. The Democrats of the time, dominant in the South, defended slavery. The Whigs for many years tried to avoid the issue as being too divisive.

By 1840 this reluctance had convinced a number of abolitionists of the need to form a party of their own to advance their cause. In that year a group of abolitionists—not including Garrison, who maintained stoutly that the force of argument alone would defeat slavery—formed the Liberty Party and nominated James G. Birney for president. The party did poorly in the 1840 election but fared much better in 1844, when Birney was again its nominee.

Four years later the appeal of an abolitionist party was much stronger. By then the Whigs had divided on the slavery question; the faction known as Conscience Whigs opposed slavery, whereas the Cotton Whigs wanted to continue to duck the issue. Northern Democrats, similarly, were split into two factions—the Barnburners, who opposed the effort to extend slavery into new states, and the Hunkers, who felt the party should not antagonize its supporters in the South. In 1848 the Barnburners, the Conscience Whigs and the leaders of the Liberty Party met to form a new antislavery party, which called itself the Free Soil Party. Its main goal was to keep slavery from spreading to new states. With former President Martin Van Buren as its nominee for president, the party did well in the election of 1848, electing 13 members to Congress. The results showed that the people who believed in political action to abolish slavery were gaining strength.

Their position grew stronger as a result of the Kansas-Nebraska Act of 1854—the law that allowed new territories about to become states to decide the slavery issue for themselves and gave rise to the fierce struggle over that issue in Kansas. To many Northerners, the law meant that the battle over extending slavery to new states would go on indefinitely. The law had split the Whig Party so sharply between northern and southern factions that it was no longer an effective organization. The time was ripe for a new party that would stand clearly against slavery. Northern Whigs, former supporters of the Liberty and Free Soil parties, northern Democrats against the extension of slavery and many other people who had come to hold the views of the abolitionists were ready to support such a party. It was in this climate that the Republican Party, organized in Wisconsin early in 1854, quickly became the major political voice of the antislavery movement.

By 1856 the battle over whether Kansas should be a free state or a slave state had brought the issue of slavery to the center of the political stage. The issue was put in a bright spotlight by a shocking and unprecedented event that took place on the afternoon of May 22.

Three days earlier, Senator Charles Sumner of Massachusetts—a man of strong antislavery views—began a long speech in the Senate on the "Crime of Kansas." (It happened to be the day that the proslavery mob from Missouri attacked Lawrence, Kansas, destroying a new hotel and burning several homes.) The crime of Sumner's theme was "the rape of a virgin Territory [Kansas], compelling it to the full embrace of slavery; and it may be clearly traced to a depraved longing for a new Slave State, the hideous offspring of such a crime, in the hope of adding to the power of Slavery in the National Government." But Sumner also directed some sharp and personal remarks at three proslavery senators: Stephen A. Douglas of Illinois, Andrew P. Butler of South Carolina and James M. Mason of Virginia.

In the tradition of the Senate, he did not mention the senators by name but by title and state. "The Senator from South Carolina," he said, "overflowed with rage at the simple suggestion that Kansas had applied for admission as a State; and . . . discharged the loose expectoration of his speech, now upon her representative, and then upon her people. There was no . . . possible deviation from truth which he did not make. . . . "

Representative Preston S. Brooks of South Carolina, a nephew of Butler, was a man who upheld the Southern tradition of avenging what he saw as personal insults. He pondered what to do to avenge Sumner's remarks about Butler.

When the Senate adjourned for the day on May 22, Sumner remained at his desk, working on some papers. Brooks entered the Senate chamber, carrying a gold-handled cane, and went to Sumner's desk. "I have read your speech twice over carefully," he said. "It is a libel on South Carolina, and Mr. Butler, who is a relative of mine." Then Brooks began beating Sumner savagely with the cane. Sumner was seriously injured, with deep cuts on his head and welts on his arms and legs.

The attack stunned the North. Newspapers railed at the lengths to which Southerners would go to defend slavery. Rallies were held to condemn the brutality of the attack. Southerners cheered Brooks. The Richmond *Inquirer* said: "We consider his act good in conception, better in execution, and best of all in consequence. The vulgar Abolitionists in the Senate are getting above themselves." Several people sent canes to Brooks, implying that he should beat some more abolitionists. When he resigned from Congress after being censured by the House of Representatives, the voters of his congressional district promptly reelected him, casting only six votes against him.

With the battle over slavery approaching a boil, the U.S. Supreme Court added fuel to the fire with its decision in the case of *Dred Scott v. Sandford*. (Court officials made a rare mistake by misspelling the name of the defendant; it was *Sanford,* but the misspelling has gone down in history.) Dred Scott had been a slave, owned by Dr. John Emerson of Missouri. Emerson was a surgeon in the U.S. Army, and in his travels with the Army he had taken Scott to Illinois (a free state) and Wisconsin (a free territory under the Missouri Compromise) before returning with him to Missouri. When Emerson died, his widow transferred Scott to her brother, John F. A. Sanford of New York.

Scott sued for his freedom, claiming that his residence in a free state and a free territory had lifted him out of slavery. The case dragged on in the courts for years, until in March 1857 the Supreme

Charles Sumner was an abolitionist United States senator from Massachusetts. A speech he made in the Senate in 1856 attacked a slave-state senator, Andrew P. Butler of South Carolina. Three days later Representative Preston S. Brooks of South Carolina, Senator Butler's nephew, entered the Senate chamber and beat Sumner savagely with a cane. The episode provoked great outrage in the North and heightened the tensions that culminated in the Civil War.

Court ruled that Scott remained a slave because the Constitution did not recognize slaves as citizens of the U.S. and only citizens had the right to sue in federal courts.

That finding alone probably would not have stirred much furor, but the Court took another step. It ruled that the Missouri Compromise was illegal because the Constitution did not give Congress power to regulate slavery in the territories. In other words, slavery could exist in all the territories.

People in the North read this decision to mean that the South could move to force slavery anywhere. Newspapers thundered against the Court and the supporters of slavery. Dred Scott Indignation meetings were held in many places, attended by large numbers of people who were new to the antislavery cause.

Into this explosive atmosphere hurtled the firebrand John Brown. Brought up in a strictly religious household, he had rigid views of what was right and what was wrong. Slavery was wrong. As a young man, he led a number of violent guerrilla attacks against supporters of slavery. One of them was a massacre of five proslavery men in Kansas in revenge for the sacking of Lawrence, Kansas, and the caning of Charles Sumner on the same day in 1856.

By 1857, Brown was in Boston, lining up financial and moral support among leading abolitionists for a bigger scheme. He had decided that an attack in the South would induce masses of slaves to rise up in revolt against slavery. After a prolonged study of maps of southern territory, he decided that the target to attack was the federal arsenal at Harpers Ferry in Virginia. His plan was to capture the arsenal, thereby gaining a large supply of weapons and ammunition for the hordes of slaves who would join his crusade. He was so confident of success that he drew up a constitution for the territory he and his slave army would conquer.

Brown chose the night of October 16, 1859, for his attack. His force consisted of 18 men. They descended on the arsenal, overpowering the night watchman easily. But they also captured a few townspeople who were about, and that made word of the attack spread quickly. A force of townspeople rushed to counterattack. Brown sent his son Watson and another man out with a white flag to talk of truce; the furious townspeople killed them both. Within hours, President Buchanan had dispatched federal troops under the command of Col. Robert E. Lee. Brown and most of his small remaining force were captured. Brought to trial a week later, Brown was convicted of conspiracy, treason and murder and sentenced to hang.

John Brown, a militant abolitionist, led a raid on the federal arsenal at Harpers Ferry, Virginia, on October 16, 1859. He believed that an attack on the South at that explosive time before the Civil War would inspire large numbers of slaves to rise in revolt against slavery. The raid was poorly planned and executed and was quickly put down by federal troops, but it had a tremendous impact on the South because many people there thought it would prompt further attacks by abolitionists. Brown was convicted of conspiracy, treason and murder and was hanged on December 2.

In terms of planning and execution, Brown's raid was a farce. But it had a tremendous impact on the country. Southerners were convinced that it signaled further attempts by abolitionists to foment slave rebellions. Northerners treated Brown as a hero. On December 2, the day of his execution, church bells tolled in the North and guns were fired in salute to him and his sacrifice to the abolitionist cause.

CHAPTER FOUR NOTES

page 38   "usually monotonous . . . " Quoted in the **Dictionary of American Biography.** New York: Charles Scribner's Sons, 1960, vol. IV, part 1, p. 171.

page 38   "till every chain . . . " **The Liberator,** January 1, 1831, p. 1.

page 38   "I will be . . . " **The Liberator,** January 1, 1831, p. 1.

page 39   "The truth is . . . " *Gilbert H. Barnes,* **The Anti-Slavery Impulse, 1830–1844.** Gloucester, Mass.: P. Smith, 1957, p. 50.

page 41   "The object of this Society . . . " Quoted in *Francine Klagsbrun,* **Freedom Now!,** p. 45.

page 41   "That is a providential man! . . ." Quoted in *Francine Klagsbrun,* **Freedom Now!,** p. 38.

page 41   "Ought the people . . . " Quoted in *Louis Filler,* **The Crusade Against Slavery,** p. 69.

page 42   "TWENTY DOLLARS REWARD. . . ." *Theodore D. Weld,* **American Slavery As It Is.** New York: Arno Press, 1968, p. 152.

page 42   "I took an almost malicious satisfaction . . . " Quoted in *Francine Klagsbrun,* **Freedom Now!,** p. 108.

page 42   "I stand before you . . . " Quoted in *Francine Klagsbrun,* **Freedom Now!,** p. 111.

page 44   "Massachusetts Abolition University . . . " Quoted in *Francine Klagsbrun,* **Freedom Now!,** p. 84.

page 46   "wicked plan . . . " Quoted in *Francine Klagsbrun,* **Freedom Now!,** p. 78.

page 46   "prohibit . . . the circulation . . . " *James D. Richardson* (editor), **Messages and Papers of the Presidents.** New York: Bureau of National Literature and Art, 1896–1904, vol. III, p. 176.

page 47   "friends of the Union." Quoted in *Francine Klagsbrun,* **Freedom Now!,** p. 55.

page 47   "to take you . . . " Quoted in *Francine Klagsbrun,* **Freedom Now!,** pp. 57–58.

page 47   "a shock . . . " Quoted in *Francine Klagsbrun,* **Freedom Now!,** p. 81.

page 49   "slavery and involuntary servitude . . . " Act of Congress, March 6, 1820; vol. 3, United States Statutes, p. 545.

page 51   "gone off . . . " Quoted in *John Hope Franklin,* **From Slavery to Freedom,** p. 255.

page 51   "One of the most interesting . . . " Quoted in *Herbert Aptheker,* **A Documentary History of the Negro People in the United States,** vol. 1, p. 277.

page 54   "from this hour . . . " *Harriet Beecher Stowe,* **Uncle Tom's Cabin.** New York: The Library of America, 1982, p. 489.

page 54   "This was the book . . . " *Philip Van Doren Stern,* **The Annotated Uncle Tom's Cabin.** New York: P.S. Eriksson, 1964, p. 7.

page 55   "Within its pestilential atmosphere . . . " Quoted in
          Louis Filler, **The Crusade Against Slavery,** p. 255.

page 56   "the rape . . . " Quoted in *N. W. Senior,* **American
          Slavery.** London: Longmans, 1856, p. 72.

page 56   "The Senator from South Carolina . . . " Quoted in *N. W.
          Senior,* **American Slavery,** p. 76.

page 57   "I have read . . . " Quoted in *N. W. Senior,* **American
          Slavery,** p. 153.

page 57   "We consider . . . " Quoted in *N. W. Senior,* **American
          Slavery,** p. 155.

CHAPTER Five

WAR
The Union Breaks Up

Brown's raid and the growing chorus of Northern voices calling for an end to slavery inflamed the South. People there talked increasingly of leaving the Union that no longer seemed hospitable. When the young Republican Party's nominee Abraham Lincoln won the presidential election of 1860, the South could see that slavery would come under even more pressure. South Carolina decided on secession within weeks of the election, declaring in December 1860 that the union between South Carolina and other states under the name of The United States of America was at an end. By the time of Lincoln's inauguration on March 4, 1861, Georgia, Alabama, Florida, Mississippi, Louisiana and Texas had followed South Carolina into secession and had formed the Confederate States of America. They were soon joined by Arkansas, North Carolina, Tennessee and Virginia.

Alexander Stephens, vice president of the Confederacy, put the new government's position squarely. Speaking in Savannah, Georgia, in 1861, he attacked Thomas Jefferson and the other founders of the Union who had held that all men are created equal and that slavery was wrong. Said Stephens:

> Our new Government is founded upon exactly the opposite ideas; its foundations are laid, its corner stone rests upon the great truth that the negro is not equal to the white man; that slavery, subordination to the superior race, is his natural and normal condition.

Lincoln quickly faced a crisis. The Confederate states had quietly taken over most of the federal property in their territory, but U.S. forces still controlled Fort Sumter, which stood on an island in the harbor at Charleston, South Carolina. When President Buchanan had tried in January 1861 to deliver reinforcements and supplies to the fort, Confederate guns on the shore had fired at and driven off the ship carrying them. That incident could have been treated as an act of war, but Buchanan chose not to make an issue of it. Now, in April, the commander of the fort—Major Robert Anderson—told Washington he could not hold out without reinforcements.

Most of Lincoln's advisers urged him to pull the federal forces out of the fort. Lincoln thought that would amount to a recognition of the Confederacy, which he had declared to be illegal and insurrectionary. He told the government of South Carolina that he would reprovision the fort. The Confederate response was to summon Anderson and demand that he surrender the fort. He refused. That same day, April 12, the Confederate guns opened fire on the fort, forcing its surrender. From that day forward, it was plain to both abolitionists in the North and whites in the South that the issues of slavery and secession would be settled only by war. The war was on.

Oddly, it was not so plain to many other Northerners that slavery was at issue in the war. They accepted the idea that slaves were property and that property should be respected. The *New York Tribune* declared in May 1861 that "this War is in truth a War for the preservation of the Union, not for the destruction of Slavery; and it would alienate many ardent Unionists to pervert it into a war against Slavery." Lincoln himself insisted early in the war that the issue was the preservation of the Union. "My paramount object in this struggle is to save the Union," he said in 1862, "and is not either to save or to destroy slavery. If I could save the Union without freeing any slave, I would do it; and if I could save it by freeing all the slaves, I would do it; and if I could do it by freeing some and leaving others alone, I would also do that."

It soon became clear, however, that while slavery may not have been the *key* issue for Northerners, it was nonetheless of great importance. It was, after all, the reason the Confederate states had left the Union. Moreover, it was to the military advantage of the

North to disrupt slavery—the labor force on which the Southern economy depended. Henry W. Halleck, general-in-chief of the Union army, put the case pointedly in 1863. Writing to General Ulysses S. Grant, then commander of the Union effort to gain control of the Mississippi River, Halleck said:

Genl, It is the policy of the government to withdraw from the enemy as much productive labor as possible. So long as the rebels retain and employ their slaves in producing grains, &c, they can employ all the whites in the field [as soldiers]. Every slave withdrawn from the enemy, is equivalent to a white man put hors de combat [out of action].

Southern whites saw the situation of the slaves from a different perspective. Their concern was that with white men going off to war, the slaves would strike for freedom. William H. Lee, a farmer in Bells Landing, Alabama, wrote about it to Jefferson Davis, the president of the Confederate States:

Dear Sir   i havs to in form you that thire is a good many pore men with large famely to susport An if they have to go in to the Army there famelys will sufer thire is a Nother question to rise with us the Negroes is very Hiley Hope up that they will soon Be free so i think you Had Better order out All the Negroe felers from 17 years oald up Ether fort them up or put them in the army and Make them fite like good fels for wee ar in danger of our lives hear among them

A more literate Southern white, John J. Cheatham of Georgia, put the viewpoint more fully in a letter to the Confederate secretary of war:

Some of our people are fearful that when a large portion of our fighting men are taken from the country, that large numbers of our negroes aided by emissaries will ransack portions of the country, kill numbers of our inhabitants, and make their way to the black republicans; There is no doubt but that Lincoln's intention is to set them all free. Then, to counteract this idea, and make them assist in whipping the black republicans, which by the by would be the best thing that could be done, could they not be incorporated into our armies, say ten or twenty placed promiscuously in each company? In this way there number would be too small to do our army any injury, whilst they might be made quite efficient in battle, as there are a great many I have no doubt that would make good soldiers and would willingly go if they had a chance. They might be valued as you would a horse or other property, and let the government pay for them if they was killed in battle. . . .

A few slaves were taken into service with the Confederate army. That policy backfired in a way that one such enlisted slave described to the Southern Claims Commission in 1873:

My name is Samuel Elliott I was born in Liberty County [Georgia] a Slave and became free when the [Union] Army came into the County. I belonged to Maybank Jones. I am 54 years old. I reside at Laurelview in Liberty County. I am a farmer. . . .

I resided from the 1st of April 1861 to the 1st of June 1865 where I live now at Laurelview. I worked for my master all the time. I changed my business at one time when I was with my master as a waiter—in the rebel service I was with him Eleven month. I came home with him. I told my son what was going on—he with 11 more ran off and joined the Army (the Yankee Army) on St Catherine Island. I dont remember the Year but it was soon after the battle at Williamsburgh Va, and before the 7 days battle near Chickahomony. I mean that was the time when I came home with my master. I was with him at Yorktown—Soon after I came home My son with 11 others ran away and joined the Union Army. My master had me taken up tied me and tried to make me tell "What made them ran off" I had to lie about it to keep from getting killed. the 11 slaves belonged to My Master Jones that stoped the slave owners from sending or taking slave into the Army or anything else. it stoped it in our neighborhood

The slaves did not strike for freedom, but they were quick to seize opportunities to escape from their masters whenever Union troops came close. The flow of slaves into Union camps caused problems for Union commanders. General Benjamin F. Butler, the commander at Fortress Monroe in Virginia, described the problems in a letter to General-in-Chief Winfield Scott:

> Since I wrote my last dispatch the question in regard to slave property is becoming one of very serious magnitude. The [rebel] inhabitants of Virginia are using their negroes in the batteries, and are preparing to send the women and children South. The escapes from them are very numerous, and a squad has come in this morning [May 27, 1861] to my pickets bringing their women and children. Of course these cannot be dealt with upon the Theory on which I designed to treat the services of able bodied men and women who come into my lines. . . . I am in the utmost doubt what to do with this species of property. . . . I have therefore determined to employ, as I can do very profitably, the able-bodied persons in the party, issuing proper food for the support of all, and charging against their services the expense and care and sustenance of the non-laborers. . . .

Scott supported Butler, and so did Secretary of War Simon Cameron. Butler proceeded with enthusiasm, calling the runaway slaves "contraband of war." He meant that as enemy property they could be kept by Union troops as a means of weakening the Confederacy. Fugitive slaves, increasing in number, soon became widely known in the North as "contrabands." In August 1861 Congress adopted the First Confiscation Act, which made slaves and other Confederate property the "subject of prize and capture wherever found."

As one can imagine, making it to freedom in a Union camp was an exhilirating experience for the runaways. Few of them were in a position to put their feelings in writing, but John Boston, a slave from Maryland who took refuge in a regiment from New York, probably spoke for them all in a letter to the wife he had to leave behind:

> it is with grate joy I take this time to let you know Whare I am i am now in Safety in the 14th Regiment of Brooklyn this Day i can Adress you thank god as a free man I had a little truble in giting away But as the lord led the Children of Israel to the land of Canon So he led me to a land Whare fredom will rain in spite Of earth and hell

The slaveowners saw the situation of the contrabands differ-ently. They thought the Union troops should return the slaves to their owners, particularly when an owner personally went into a Union camp and asked for the return of slaves he knew were there. A. J. Smoot of Maryland described his attempt to secure the return of his slaves in a letter to the Maryland legislature:

On or about the 14th of november last [1861] I proceeded to Camp Fenton near Port Tobacco to get three of my servants viz a man about Twenty four years of age a boy about seventeen years of age and a boy some 13 or 14 years of age who had left their home and taken up their abode with the soldiers at the above named camp. Col. Graham who was in command at the time gave me an order to the officer of the day to search the camp for my servants but at the same time intimated I might meet with some difficulty as a portion of his troops were abolitionist I learned by some of the soldiers my servants were in Camp and soon as my mission became general known a large crowd collected and followed me crying shoot him, bayonet him, kill him, pitch him out, the nigger Stealer the nigger driver at first their threats were accompanied by a few stones thrown at me which very soon became an allmost continued shower of stones a number of which struck me, but did me no serious damage. Seeing the officer who accompanied me took no notice of what was going on and fearing that some of the soldiers would put their threats of shooting me into execution I informed him that I would not proceed any farther, about this time Lieutenant Edmund Harrison came to my assistance and swore he would shoot the first man who threw a stone at me, the soldiers hooted at him and continued throwing. I returned to Col Grahams headquarters but was not permitted to see him again. I left the camp without getting my servants and have not been favored to get them yet

The flow of contrabands and agitation in the North put Lin-coln under increasing pressure to free the slaves. Congress in-creased the pressure by passing a bill freeing the slaves in the District of Columbia. Lincoln signed the bill into law in April 1862. Besides freeing the slaves, it provided $100,000 "to aid in the colonization and settlement" of any freed blacks in the District of

Columbia "as may desire to emigrate to the Republics of Haiti or Liberia, or such other country beyond the limits of the United States."

This law gave rise to a remarkable petition to Congress from 40 black men who had been freed by the law. Their main aim was to get help in moving to another country, but what they said underscored the predicament of freed slaves and foreshadowed some of the problems that freedom would bring:

> *The undersigned, for themselves, their relatives, and friends, whom they represent; desire, by this memorial, most respectfully to show to the Congress and people of this great country—of which, too, they are natives, but humbly born—that they appreciate, to the fullest extent,*

Toward the end of the Civil War, the federal government established the Freedmen's Bureau to help the freed slaves adjust to their new life. A large part of the bureau's work was education, since few slaves knew how to read or write. This sketch of "the Misses Cooke's school room," operated by the Freedmen's Bureau in Richmond, appeared in *Frank Leslie's Illustrated Newspaper* in 1866.

*the humane actions which are now inaugurated to give
freedom to their so long oppressed colored race; but they
believe that this freedom will result injuriously, unless
there shall be opened to colored people a region, to
which they may immigrate—a country which is suited to
their organization, and in which they may seek and
secure, by their own industry, that mental and physical
industry, that mental and physical development which
will allow them an honorable position in the families of
God's great world.*

*That there is ignorance in the mass of the colored
race, is not to be denied: this is caused by the peculiar
condition in which they have been raised—without the
advantages of general education so wisely and freely
accorded to the white citizens. But there are those
amongst them who have secured the blessings of
knowledge, and who are capable of informing their
brethren of what is for their ultimate good. . . .*

By late 1862, Lincoln had made up his mind to take a bigger
step toward freeing the slaves when the military situation was
ripe. That time came in September, when Union forces had captured significant amounts of Confederate territory and slaves
were coming over the Union lines in droves. Lincoln announced
on September 22 that he would issue an emancipation proclamation on January 1, 1863. As issued on that day, it applied to the 11
states then in rebellion but not to the border states—Missouri,
Kentucky, Maryland and Delaware—which permitted slavery
but were fighting on the Union side. The proclamation said that
"all persons held as slaves" in the rebelling states "are, and
henceforward shall be, free." That declaration did not actually free
anyone immediately, but as the Union armies took more and more
Confederate territory, more and more slaves became free men and
women.

The kind of turmoil that freedom for slaves created in the
South was suggested by John C. P. Wederstrandt, who owned a
sugar plantation near New Orleans. The area had come under
Union control, and in September 1862 Wederstrandt wrote to the
Union general serving as military governor:

*On Monday last, while on a visit to my plantation, I was
startled at the dawn of day by the announcement of my*

*brother in law Mr Smith the manager of the place, that
the negroes were in a state of insurection, some of them
refusing to work— Proceeding immediately to the Cabin
Yard, I found them gathered in different groups & on
enquiry learned, that some of them would not work at
all, & others wanted wages, I informed them, I should not
pay wages, & being excited by their ingratitude & not
wishing to feed and clothe those who would not work, &
to avoid any difficulty, as my sister and her four small
children were on the place, I said that it was better to
part in peace & go off quietly & that I did not wish to lay
eyes on them again, & they went away*

Worn down, with its economy in disarray, the Confederacy
surrendered in April 1865. The war was over. The question of what
to do about putting the Union back together and arranging a new
life for the four million freed slaves was at hand.

Many freed slaves in the South soon found themselves
returned to a state that closely resembled slavery. Arrested,
often on a trumped-up charge, the former slave would be
turned over to a white man who paid the fine—in effect
buying the prisoner. Charged for room and board as well as
for the amount of the fine, the black man found that he could
never quite pay off his debt.

CHAPTER FIVE NOTES

page 65   "Our new Government . . . " Quoted in *James M. McPherson*, **The Struggle for Equality,** p. 61.

page 66   "this War . . . " Quoted in *James M. McPherson,* **The Struggle for Equality,** p. 56.

page 66   "My paramount object . . . " *Abraham Lincoln*, letter to Horace Greeley, August 22, 1862.

page 67   "Genl, It is the policy . . . " Quoted in *Ira Berlin* et al. (editors), **Free at Last,** p. 101.

page 67   "Dear Sir . . . " Quoted in *Ira Berlin* et al. (editors), **Free at Last,** p.4.

page 67   "Some of our people . . . " Quoted in *Ira Berlin* et al. (editors), **Free at Last,** p. 5.

page 68   "My name is . . . " Quoted in *Ira Berlin*, et al. (editors), **Free at Last,** p.60.

page 69   "Since I wrote . . . " Quoted in *Ira Berlin* et al. (editors), **Free at Last,** p. 9.

page 69   "it is with grate joy . . . " Quoted in *Ira Berlin* et al. (editors), **Free at Last,** p.29.

page 70   "On or about the 14th of november . . . " Quoted in *Ira Berlin* et al. (editors), **Free at Last,** p. 33.

page 71   "The undersigned . . . " Quoted in *Ira Berlin* et al. (editors), **Free at Last,** p.39.

page 72   "all persons . . . " *Abraham Lincoln*, Emancipation Proclamation, January 1, 1863.

page 72   "On Monday last . . . " Quoted in *Ira Berlin*, et al. (editors), **Free at Last,** p. 72.

CHAPTER Six

RECONSTRUCTION
Rebuilding the South and the Nation

It was plain early in the war that serious problems of rebuilding the disrupted Union and helping the freed slaves find a footing would have to be dealt with when the war ended. The word applied to the task then and thereafter was "Reconstruction." Indeed, the first move came as early as 1862, after Union forces had captured New Orleans. General Benjamin Butler, the Union commander, proposed to readmit Louisianans as citizens of the United States if they took a simple oath of allegiance to the national government. President Lincoln neither accepted nor rejected this plan, so Butler went ahead on his own. By August, 11,000 people had taken the oath. It was they who shortly afterward elected two men to the United States House of Representatives. Reconstruction was under way. It became a major operation when the war ended in 1865.

The changed atmosphere in the South was evident in an episode that took place in Mobile, Alabama, late in 1865. T. Kilby Smith, the Union general who was overseeing the reconstruction program there, received a visit from a prominent woman. He later told a Senate committee about it:

One of the most high-bred ladies of Mobile, having had silver plate stolen from her more than two years ago, and having, upon affidavit [a statement made under oath], secured the incarceration of two of her former slaves whom she suspected of the theft, came to me in my

official capacity, and asked my order to have them
whipped and tortured into a confession. . . . This lady
was surprised when I informed her that the days of the
rack and the thumbscrew were passed. . . . I offer this as
an instance of the feeling that exists in all classes against
the negro, and their inability to realize that he is a free
man and entitled to the rights of citizenship.

There, in a nutshell, was the problem. It was easy enough to end slavery, but securing equal rights for free blacks was going to take a long time. The fate of slavery was sealed quickly. Before the war ended, Congress had presented to the states a 13th amendment to the Constitution, declaring that "neither slavery nor involuntary servitude . . . shall exist within the United States." Enough states approved the amendment to make it part of the Constitution by the end of 1865. But the end of slavery was the beginning of the problem of what to do about the freed slaves— most of them illiterate, desperately poor and without experience of life as free people.

Lincoln had thought about the problems of the postwar period long before the end of the war. His idea was to avoid rancor and vengefulness by letting the rebellious states back into the Union on moderate terms. The federal government would make arrangements to look after the well-being of the freed slaves, to help educate them and to give the vote to at least the better educated among them. This program, in Lincoln's view, was to be established and carried out by the president. Therein lay the seeds of trouble, for powerful men in Congress thought otherwise. The power to lay out the plans for dealing with the rebellious states and the freed slaves, they said, rested with Congress.

The struggle began before the war ended. In December 1863, Lincoln issued what he called a Proclamation of Amnesty and Reconstruction. It offered pardon to most Confederates if they took an oath to support the United States. When a fairly small number of people in a state (equal to one-tenth of the number who had voted in the presidential election of 1860) had done that and had established a state government, he would readmit the state to the Union. Lincoln revealed later his plan for blacks: "The restoration of the Rebel States to the Union must rest upon the principle of civil and political equality of both races."

That plan was too mild for Congress, which in 1864 passed a law requiring a majority of whites in a Confederate state to take the oath before the state could rejoin the Union. The sponsors of the bill also delivered a rebuke to Lincoln, telling him he "must understand . . . that the authority of Congress is paramount."

Who would have prevailed in this contest is impossible to say, because the war had scarcely ended before Lincoln was dead. Shot by the actor John Wilkes Booth while attending a performance at Ford's Theater in Washington on April 14, 1865, Lincoln died the next morning. The task of dealing with Congress over Reconstruction fell to Lincoln's successor, Andrew Johnson.

Johnson was a Southerner and a Democrat, but he had supported the Union side and so was made the Republican nominee for vice president in 1864 to broaden the party's appeal. On becoming president, he said he would carry out Lincoln's plan for restoring Confederate states to the Union. But he was not sympathetic to the idea that the federal government should enforce civil rights for the freed slaves. That power, he said, lay with the states. The stage was set for a collision between the new president and a Congress bent on taking charge of Reconstruction.

Johnson kept his course by pardoning former Confederate leaders, making them eligible to vote in setting up new state governments. He would then propose to let the state back into the Union. Congress would refuse to seat the people the state had elected to the House and Senate.

By December 1865, all the former Confederate states except Texas had been reorganized under Johnson's plan. Former Confederate leaders dominated the state governments. Those governments began to pass black codes that kept the free blacks almost as downtrodden as they had been as slaves. Typically, blacks with no visible means of support were declared to be vagrants. They could be arrested, fined and turned over to people who would pay the fines. That returned them to a condition closely resembling slavery. Similar treatment befell blacks who by act, word or gesture offended a white person. In some states, blacks were not allowed inside town limits without a special permit. South Carolina would not allow blacks to take any jobs except in farming and household work unless they had a special permit.

During the same period, organized bands of whites began terrorizing blacks throughout the South. The guiding spirit was what has been called "the ignoble hate and cruel itch to take him [the Negro] in hand which for so long had been festering impotently in the poor whites." From the viewpoint of a black person, it was hard to see that the war had changed anything.

The federal government was trying to help freed slaves during this period. In the closing days of the Civil War, Congress had set up the Bureau of Refugees, Freedmen, and Abandoned Lands, which quickly became known as the Freedmen's Bureau. It provided the freed slaves with food, clothing and medical services. It also set up schools to overcome the lack of education that was such a handicap to most of them. As one might expect, Southern whites viewed the Freedmen's Bureau and its works with loathing and did what they could to resist and undermine its efforts.

All this was too much for Congress, particularly the strong faction that was becoming known as the Radical Republicans. It seemed to them that Reconstruction as it proceeded under Johnson was giving the Confederates back what they had lost in the war. Thaddeus Stevens, a congressman from Pennsylvania, was among the most outspoken of the Radical Republicans. "Dead states," he thundered, "cannot restore their existence. The future condition of the conquered power depends on the will of the conqueror. . . . Congress must create [Southern] states and declare when they are entitled to be represented."

From then on, it was war between Johnson and Congress. In 1866, Congress passed a law extending the life of the Freedmen's Bureau, enlarging its power and putting much of the South under military control. Johnson vetoed it. Congress then passed a civil rights bill containing many of the same provisions and going on to declare that blacks were citizens of the United States. Johnson vetoed it. Congress passed it over his veto.

Johnson did nothing to enforce the law. Congress thereupon adopted what was to become the 14th Amendment to the Constitution, which went further than the law. It declared "all persons born or naturalized in the United States" to be citizens of the United States and of their state and forbade the states to pass any law limiting the rights of citizens or denying anyone "the equal protection of the laws."

Congress adopted the amendment in June 1866 and sent it to the states. By the end of the year, every Southern state except Tennessee had rejected it or failed to vote on it. Since the Radicals in Congress insisted that a state would have to approve the amendment and give blacks the vote before returning to the Union, most of the former Confederacy remained in limbo.

This situation prompted the Radicals to take a stronger hand with the South. In 1867, they pushed through Congress the First Reconstruction Act, which put the "rebel" states under military control and declared that they would have to approve the 14th Amendment and give all adult males the vote before they could reenter the Union. Johnson vetoed the law, saying:

> *The purpose and object of the bill—the general intent which pervades it from beginning to end—is to change the entire character of the State governments and to compel them by force to the adoption of organic laws and regulations which they are unwilling to accept if left to themselves. The Negroes have not asked for the privilege of voting; the vast majority of them have no idea what it means.*

Congress passed the law over the veto and got the results it wanted. Between April and July of 1868, Arkansas, Florida, North Carolina, Louisiana, South Carolina, Alabama and Georgia fell into line and approved the 14th Amendment. That was enough to put the amendment in the Constitution and bring those states back into the Union.

With the battle over the Reconstruction Act, the Radicals had had enough of Johnson. On what amounted to a pretext, they persuaded the House of Representatives to impeach him—that is, to declare that he had committed high crimes and misdemeanors. (The official charge was that he had violated the Tenure of Office Act of 1867 by removing the secretary of war, Edwin M. Stanton, without the consent of the Senate.)

The Senate tries impeachments and, by a vote of two-thirds, can remove the impeached person from office. Johnson came to trial in 1868. On May 10, the Senate voted against him by 35 to 10.

That was one vote short of the required two-thirds of the members present. Johnson had survived, but for the 10 months remaining in his term he avoided further battles with Congress.

Black men could now vote in the South. Ironically, the vote in much of the North was still restricted to white men. Indeed, as late as 1867, New Jersey and Ohio rejected moves toward Negro suffrage. Black men were granted the right to vote everywhere in 1870, however, with the adoption of the 15th Amendment: "The right of citizens of the United States to vote shall not be denied or abridged by the United States or by any State on account of race, color, or previous condition of servitude." Women, white or black, did not get the vote until the 19th Amendment was adopted in 1920, after a struggle almost as long and heated as the antislavery movement.

With the vote, and with federal troops backing them up, blacks began to make their mark in the state governments formed on the terms laid down by the Radicals. Louisiana, Mississippi and South Carolina had black lieutenant governors. The speaker of the house in Mississippi and the superintendent of education in Florida were blacks. Between 1869 and 1901, 22 blacks from the South were elected to Congress. Two black men—Hiram R. Revels and Blanche K. Bruce (a former slave)—served as senators from Mississippi. Of the 20 blacks elected to the House of Representatives, eight came from South Carolina, four from North Carolina, three from Alabama and one each from Florida, Georgia, Louisiana, Mississippi and Virginia.

But the success of blacks in the South, and of Radical Reconstruction, did not last long. It could not be expected that Southern whites would lie down and let Reconstruction roll over them. Above all, they wanted to make sure that blacks did not vote even though the law said they could. Among the many groups organized by whites to terrorize blacks, one soon became a fearsome power throughout the South. It was the Ku Klux Klan, formed in Tennessee in 1865. (The strange name perhaps came from the Greek *kirkos*, the root of "circle.") The historian John Hope Franklin tells what followed:

> In the spring of 1867 delegates from several states met in convention at Nashville, placed [Confederate] General Nathan B. Forrest at the head of the organization as the

Grand Wizard, and sent its members back to their homes fired with a determination to nullify the program of congressional reconstruction that was just getting under way. No longer was it sufficient to frighten or terrorize Negroes by ghoulish dress, weird rituals, and night rides. By social and business ostracism of the white Radicals, by intimidation and any effective means of violence conceivable against Negroes, by the purchase of votes of any sellers and by glorifying the white race and especially white womanhood, the Klan grimly moved to wreck each and every phase of Radical Reconstruction.

Several of the reconstructed states passed "Ku Klux Klan" laws in an effort to bring the Klan and other secret societies under control. They did not succeed. By 1870, the lawlessness and violence of these groups had put the entire Radical Reconstruction program on the brink of collapse in many parts of the South and torn the recently won rights of blacks to shreds.

The Ku Klux Klan, an organization of white supremacists that was a scourge of blacks in the South at the time of the Civil War, was revived in 1915 and soon became active in the North as well as the South. Its program called for "uniting native-born white Christians for concerted action in the preservation of American institutions and the supremacy of the white race." The Klan was much given to hooded white costumes and secret rituals. The photograph shows a Klan demonstration at Beckley, West Virginia, in 1924.

It was plain that the Southern states would do nothing to protect the rights of blacks to vote and to be treated fairly under the law. In fact, they would do everything they could to sabotage those rights. If the blacks were to get protection, it would have to come from the federal government. In December 1870, President Ulysses S. Grant declared that "a free exercise of the elective franchise [the right to vote] has been by violence and intimidation denied to citizens . . . in several of the states lately in rebellion and the verdict of the people has thereby been reversed." Congress responded with a law (the Second Enforcement Act) that put voting under the protection of supervisors of elections appointed by the Federal courts. A few months later came the Third Enforcement Act, popularly known as the Ku Klux Klan Act because it tried to rein in the activities of the Klan and other secret societies with similar aims. The law made interference with the rights of blacks a crime and gave the president power to use troops to control violence against blacks.

Congress and the president were not alone in trying to make a better life for black people. Many voices in the North and some in the South were raised in their cause. Wendell Phillips, who had been a prominent abolitionist, said in 1870: "While this generation lasts it is probable the negro will need the special sympathy of his friends. Our work is not done; we probably shall never live to see it done." When the American Anti-Slavery Society disbanded after the war, many of its members set up the National Reform League to work against "social persecution of men on account of their color."

The American Missionary Association put many of its members to work in the South to help blacks, particularly with education. Gilbert Haven, a Massachusetts abolitionist, went South as bishop of the Methodist Episcopal Church. He made a point of riding in the "Negro car" when he took a train and of entertaining black people in public places. Henry Wilson, vice president under Grant, told William Lloyd Garrison in 1874, "I fear a Counter-Revolution" and urged the surviving abolitionists to "call the battle roll anew, and arrest the reactionary movements."

James Redpath, who was secretary of a Senate committee during Reconstruction, reproached Northern whites for their part in the black plight: "We knew the Negro to be timid, unarmed, illiterate; and yet we left him in the midst of the fiercest fighters on thus planet, and expected him to rule them."

But the fierce fighters—the Southern whites—had the upper hand in the South. Few blacks dared to try to vote or to exercise their other rights when it was plain that the effort would bring them punishment and perhaps cost them their lives. The federal forces were spread too thin to offer blacks much protection. In state after state, with whites controlling the voting places, the Reconstruction governments were voted out. In their place came governments approved by the Redeemers, as the whites who had set out to undo the Radical Reconstruction called themselves. Indeed, the many schemes the Redeemers used to prevent blacks from voting also kept many poor and poorly educated whites away from the polls. The schemes included literacy tests (you had to show that you could read and understand passages from, say, the Bible), long and complicated ballots and last-minute shifts in the location of voting places. So the people who really ran things in the South as Reconstruction came apart were essentially the same ones who had been in charge before the Civil War—a fairly small group of well-to-do and well-educated whites.

Changing conditions in the nation also helped to undo Reconstruction. The South's economy improved, and many Northerners sought to take advantage of the chances to make money there. Northern whites had never been ardent supporters of blacks—against slavery, yes, but not prepared to look on blacks as equals—and so Northern support for Reconstruction measures gradually faded. The federal courts struck down many of the laws Congress had passed to enforce Reconstruction. By 1876, Reconstruction was a shambles. In that year Rutherford B. Hayes was elected president in a fiercely disputed vote. One of the things he had promised in order to attract Southern votes was that he would remove federal troops from the South. He did that soon after taking office in 1877, and that act marked the formal end of Reconstruction. Only one of its goals—the return of the Confederate states to the Union—had been achieved. The other goal—fair treatment of blacks—was as distant as ever. It was to be another seven decades before the nation would try seriously to come to grips with that problem.

CHAPTER SIX NOTES

page 75   "One of the most high-bred ladies . . . " *Walter Fleming,* **Documentary History of Reconstruction.** New York: McGraw Hill, 1966, vol. 1, p. 68.

page 76   "The restoration . . . " Quoted in *John Hope Franklin,* **Reconstruction: After the Civil War,** p. 23.

page 77   "must understand . . . " Quoted in *John Hope Franklin,* **Reconstruction: After the Civil War,** p. 21.

page 78   "the ignoble hate . . . " *Wilbur J. Cash,* **The Mind of the South,** p. 113.

page 78   "Dead states . . . " Quoted in *John Hope Franklin,* **Reconstruction: After the Civil War,** p. 54.

page 79   "The purpose . . . " *James D. Richardson* (editor), **Messages and Papers of the Presidents.** New York: Bureau of National Literature and Art, 1896–1904, vol. VI, p. 507.

page 80   "In the spring . . . " *John Hope Franklin,* **Reconstruction: After the Civil War,** pp. 154–155.

page 82   "a free exercise . . . " *James D. Richardson* (editor), **Messages and Papers of the Presidents,** vol. VII, p. 97.

page 82   "While this generation lasts . . . " Quoted in *James M. McPherson,* **The Abolitionist Legacy,** p. 13.

page 82   "social persecution . . . " Quoted in *James M. McPherson,* **The Abolitionist Legacy,** p. 13.

page 82   "I fear . . . " Quoted in *James M. McPherson,* **The Abolitionist Legacy,** p. 35.

page 82   "We knew . . . " Quoted in *James M. McPherson,* **The Abolitionist Legacy,** p. 51.

CHAPTER **Seven**

THE UNEASY PEACE

Troubled Progress Toward Civil Rights

In 1961, soon after becoming president, John F. Kennedy took note of the fact that 1963 would be the 100th anniversary of Lincoln's Emancipation Proclamation. He asked the United States Commission on Civil Rights to issue in 1963 a report on the nation's progress in civil rights for blacks during those 100 years. When the report came out, it began:

> *The rise of the American Negro from slavery to citizenship is one of the most dramatic chapters of American history. It is also a continuing process, the pace of which has at times been a national disgrace.*

Indeed, between the end of the Civil War in 1865 and the end of World War II in 1945, the story of civil rights for blacks was mostly a national disgrace. The high point—on paper—was a bill put forward in 1870 by Charles Sumner, who had returned to the Senate three years after his thrashing by Representative Preston S. Brooks. It was a measure of the difficulty people had with the idea of equality for blacks that the bill took five years to became law as the Civil Rights Act of 1875. It took no time at all for the law to be largely ignored. The law sought to give blacks "full and equal enjoyment of the accommodations, advantages, facilities, and privileges of inns, public conveyances on land and water, theaters, and other places of public amusement."

But the country was in no mood to support such a law. Northerners were largely indifferent to it, and Southerners were dead set against it. In fact, Tennessee passed in 1881 the first of the "Jim Crow" laws that soon became universal in the South. (The name comes from "Jump Jim Crow," a blackface minstrel act created in 1828 by Thomas Dartmouth ["Daddy"] Rice, a white man, and performed often by him and many imitators. Because the minstrel shows essentially made fun of blacks, the name Jim Crow gradually became a derogatory term for blacks and their segregated life.) The Jim Crow laws did exactly what the Civil Rights Act had tried to prevent, separating blacks from whites on trains, in railroad stations and eventually in schools, hotels, theaters, barber shops and restaurants. (When Arkansas adopted its version of Jim Crow in 1891, a black member of the legislature

The signs "White" and "Colored" over the two doors of this cafe in Durham, North Carolina, were typical of public buildings in the South well into the 20th century. The date of this photograph was May 1940. Note the prices of the weiners, hamburgers and lunches.

found a way to needle the whites. If they did not want to associate with blacks, he said, they should pass laws to divide the streets and sidewalks so that blacks would go on one side and whites on the other.) Many people still alive can remember the time in the South when signs saying "White" and "Colored" appeared over restroom doors and public water fountains and when blacks had to ride in the back seats of buses. That time lasted well into the 20th century.

The short life of the Civil Rights Act of 1875 ended when the Supreme Court overturned the law in 1883. The decision, in what is known as *The Civil Rights Cases*, involved a black who had tried to ride in the parlor car of a train in Tennessee and blacks in California, Kansas, Missouri and New York who had been refused such things as hotel accommodations and certain theater seats. According to the Supreme Court, the 14th Amendment to the Constitution applied only to actions by states, not to what might be done against blacks by private organizations such as railroads and theaters.

By 1890, the federal government had said in effect that Jim Crow laws were acceptable. The Interstate Commerce Commission, which regulated railroads, ruled that the railroads must provide equal accommodations for whites and blacks but that they could be separate. "Separate but equal" opened the door for Jim Crow laws in every Southern state. The facilities provided were separate but rarely equal. As the *Independent* stated, blacks paid "first-class price for third-class accommodation." (The *Independent* began in 1848 as an antislavery paper published by Henry C. Bowen, who had married Lewis Tappan's daughter. It continued well into the 20th century as a champion of civil rights for blacks.)

In 1896, the Supreme Court upheld the "separate but equal" practice in the case of *Plessy* v. *Ferguson*. If "the enforced separation of the two races stamps the colored race with a badge of inferiority," the Court said, "it is not by reason of anything found in the [Jim Crow] act, but solely because the colored race chooses to put that construction upon it. . . . If the two races are to meet upon terms of social equality, it must be the result of natural affinities, a mutual appreciation of each other's merits, and a voluntary consent of individuals. . . . Legislation is powerless to eradicate racial instincts or to abolish distinctions based upon physical differences. . . . "

While working to segregate blacks in public places, Southern whites also busied themselves making sure that blacks could not or would not vote. They were greatly helped by the retreat of the federal government from the civil rights field. In 1880, Congress passed a law forbidding the use of soldiers to enforce voting rights. Another law, passed in 1894, did away with all the earlier laws that had installed federal supervisors of elections in the South. Also abolished were the parts of the First Enforcement Act declaring that the qualifications for voting should be the same for everybody and providing punishment for anyone who tried to keep a qualified voter from voting.

With the road to the voting booth for blacks now obstructed, the Southern states moved to make sure that black voters could not even find it. Mississippi, where a majority of the population was black, took the first step in 1890. It imposed a poll tax of $2 and ruled that anyone who wanted to vote would have to show first that he could read the state constitution or understand it if it was read to him. Both hurdles were far harder for poor and poorly educated blacks to leap than for most whites. But there were poor and poorly educated whites, and so the Southern states moved to keep the polls open to them. Louisiana in 1898 became the first state to enact what became known as the "grandfather clause." It allowed the vote to anyone who was eligible to vote on January 1, 1866, or was the son or grandson of such a person, even though the voter was unable to pay the poll tax or pass the reading test. All such persons would be white, since blacks did not vote in Louisiana in 1866.

The purpose of all this was stated flatly in 1901 by Carter Glass, then a state senator in Virginia and later for many years one of Virginia's two U.S. senators. Speaking at a state convention called to do what other Southern states had done about black voting, he said:

Discrimination! Why that is exactly what we propose; that, exactly, is what this convention was elected for—to discriminate to the very extremity of permissible action under the limitations of the Federal Constitution, with a view to the elimination of every Negro voter who can be gotten rid of, legally, without materially impairing the numerical strength of the white electorate.

By 1910, every former Confederate state had managed to find some way to keep most blacks from voting. But a few blacks, mostly in counties where blacks were a majority of the population, escaped the roadblocks and got to the voting booth. To Southern whites, that meant there remained a chance that a black or a white sympathetic to blacks might be elected to public office. So the whites devised yet another roadblock: the white primary. Party candidates are chosen in primary elections, and in the South before World War II, the candidates chosen by the Democratic Party were almost certain to win in the general election. If only whites were allowed to vote in the Democratic primaries, blacks would be left with virtually no political influence. By 1930, every Southern state had a white primary.

White officials resorted to other devices to keep blacks from voting. The Social Science Institute at Fisk University recorded one of them in its *A Monthly Survey of Events and Trends in Race Relations:*

> *Rather than permit a group of Negroes to register, all offices in the Marion County [S.C.] Courthouse were closed on Monday, October 6, 1945. Negro citizens from all over the county, under the leadership of the Progressive Democratic Party, came into Marion on a date designated by F. M. Boatwright, county registration officer, as an official day for registration. When the group arrived they were informed that Mr. Boatwright was not in. A "searching party" was sent out to look for the missing registrar. It is reported that they spied him at one point, but that he quickly took to his heels. Meanwhile, the door to the office in which the prospective registrants were waiting was closed. They remained, however, for five hours. Later they learned that all offices in the building were vacated soon after they came in.*

Segregation in public places and exclusion from polling places were among the milder miseries for blacks in the postwar South. Many of them found that, regardless of the 13th Amendment, they were still slaves in fact if not in name. What put them in that condition was the system known as peonage. A black told how it worked:

> I am brought in a prisoner, go through the farce of being tried. The whole of my fine may amount to fifty dollars. A kindly appearing man will come up and pay my fine and take me to his farm to allow me to work it out. At the end of a month I find that I owe him more than I did when I went there. The debt is increased year in and year out. You would ask, "How is that?" It is simply that he is charging you more for your board, lodging and washing than they allow you for your work.

There were laws against this sort of abuse, but they had little effect. In 1903, the U.S. Department of Justice investigated peonage and found scores of cases. One result of the investigation was that federal grand juries in Alabama charged 18 men with holding blacks in peonage. Only seven of them were convicted, and they—being in Southern courts—received light sentences.

The Independent published in 1912 an account by a black woman that showed how little things had changed since the days of slavery. She told of working from 14 to 16 hours a day as a servant and nursemaid for a white family in Georgia. Her pay was $10 per month. And, she said:

> Another thing—it's a small indignity, it may be, but an indignity just the same. No white person, not even the little children just learning to talk, no white person at the South ever thinks of addressing any Negro man or woman as Mr. or Mrs., or Miss. The women are called, "Cook," or "Nurse," or "Mammy," or "Mary Jane," or "Lou," or "Dilcey," as the case might be, and men are called "Bob," or "Boy," or "Old Man," or "Uncle Bill," or "Pate." In many cases our white employers refer to us, and in our presence, too, as their "niggers." No matter what they call us—no matter what they teach their children to call us—we must tamely submit, and answer when we are called; we must enter no protest; if we did object, we should be driven out without the least ceremony, and, in applying for work in other places, we should find it very hard to procure another situation. In almost every case, when our intending employers would be looking up our record, the information would be

given by telephone or otherwise that we were "impudent," "saucy," "dishonest," and "generally unreliable . . . "

Another thing. Sometimes I have gone on the street cars or the railroad trains with the white children, and, so long as I was in charge of the children, I could sit anywhere I desired, front or back. If a white man happened to ask another white man, "What is that nigger doing in here?" and was told, "Oh, she's the nurse of those white children in front of her!" immediately there was the hush of peace. Everything was all right, so long as I was in the white man's part of the street car or in the white man's coach as a servant—a slave—but as soon as I did not present myself as a menial, and the relationship of master and servant was abolished by my not having the white children with me, I would forthwith be assigned to the "nigger" seats or the "colored people's coach."

Some Southern states actually made a business of putting blacks in a position closely resembling slavery. The technique was "convict leasing." Black prisoners were rented out to private contractors, for whom they had to work. They lived in miserable camps and worked long hours under the eyes of guards who were quick to beat misbehavers. Much of the growth of industry in the South after the Civil War rested on the cheap labor of leased convicts, many of whom went to prison only because of minor offenses or trumped-up charges.

Even so, the leased convicts may have been safer than free blacks who were seen by whites to be stepping out of line. Such a black was likely to become a victim of "lynch law." That was the brutal technique of white groups that took the law into their own hands and killed blacks who, in their view, had attacked or insulted a white or had merely been obstreperous. The usual methods of killing were a public hanging or burning at the stake.

At one time lynching of whites by whites was as common in the frontier West as it later became against blacks in the postwar South. The number of lynchings reached a peak of 255 (155 of the victims being black) in 1892. Thereafter the rate went down, but the percentage of blacks went up. From 1890 through 1899, the average number of lynchings per year was 188. In that decade, 82 percent of the lynchings were in the South and 68 percent of the victims were black. During the next decade, the average number of lynchings per year dropped to 93 but the proportions changed to 92 percent in the South and 89 percent of the victims black.

As dismaying as the figures are, the manner of lynchings was even more horrible. They became public spectacles—lynching bees—with large groups watching as the victim was first tortured and then burned or hung. "A lynching bee," the historian James M. McPherson wrote, "sometimes became the occasion for a holiday, with railroads running special trains to the event and thousands of men, women and children watching the saturnalia of mutilation, screams and burning flesh."

Scarcely less shocking was the terror in the countryside. The Ku Klux Klan, which had been dormant since Reconstruction, was revived in the South in 1915. Shortly after World War I, it put forward a program for "uniting native-born white Christians for concerted action in the preservation of American institutions and the supremacy of the white race." On this program the Klan grew within a year to more than 100,000 members—many of them in the North—who were quick to take the law into their own hands by hanging, burning, flogging and torturing blacks who stepped out of line and other people viewed by the Klan as somehow anti-American.

The tension between races broke out repeatedly in the form of race riots. Some event in a community—an action by a white or a black person that seemed offensive to the other race—would set off a battle between whites and blacks. In the years around the turn of the century, major race riots took place in eight cities: Greenwood, S.C., and Wilmington, N.C., in 1898; Statesboro, Ga., and Springfield, Ohio, in 1904; Atlanta, Ga., Greensburg, Ind., and Brownsville, Tex., in 1906; and Springfield, Ill., in 1908.

Theodore Roosevelt was president during much of this time. Although he was vigorously decisive in most matters, he seemed to waffle in cases of civil rights. The Brownsville episode of 1906 was an example. Three men were shot there, allegedly by soldiers from three all-black companies stationed at Fort Brown. Although black soldiers had fought at Roosevelt's side in the Spanish-American War, and he had praised them, he dishonorably discharged from the Army all three companies of blacks even though only a few of the soldiers, absent without leave, had taken part in the shooting.

In this and in other racial clashes, the federal government did little or nothing. Indeed, pressure from Southern members of Congress moved the government in the direction of segregation. The type of pressure was indicated by a bill that Representative James B. Aswell of Louisiana introduced in 1913 "to effect certain reforms in the civil service by segregating clerks and employees of the white race from those of African blood or descent." In the same month Representative William S. Howard of Georgia put in a bill that would have required segregation in Washington's public transportation system. These bills and others like them did not pass, but the sentiment behind them caused first the Post Office Department and then the Treasury Department to segregate their offices, lunchrooms and restrooms.

The failure of federal authorities to fill the void in civil protection created by the inaction of state and local governments brought many blacks to the view that it would take legal and political moves by blacks themselves to improve their situation. They also made the point that tolerating lawlessness and violence against blacks weakened the whole structure of law and order, endangering whites as well as blacks. The black writer John L. Love put it this way in 1899:

> In the degree that they [Southern people] stand by in
> silence and see the Negro stripped of his civil and
> political rights by a band of unscrupulous men . . . they
> compromise their own civil and political freedom, and
> put in jeopardy the industrial progress of the South. . . .
> If by a mere technicality one class of citizens can be
> deprived of the rights and immunities granted by the
> organic law of the nation, what is to prevent any other
> class from sharing the same fate?

But the lawlessness continued. The summer of 1919, less than a year after the end of World War I, saw the country's worst interracial strife. Race riots broke out in 25 cities. The worst started in Chicago on July 27 after whites at a beach stoned a black man who was swimming in water they regarded as reserved for whites. He drowned, and although it was evident later that he had not been hit by the stones, the event served to set off an explosion in the tense racial atmosphere. The riots raged through the streets of Chicago for 13 days, leaving a grim tally: 15 whites and 23 blacks killed, 148 whites and 342 blacks injured and more than 1,000 families—most of them black—left homeless because of the fires that were set and the property that was destroyed by rioters.

Those blacks, and most black people in every community, lived in neighborhoods that had few whites or none. The Rev. Francis J. Grimké, pastor of the Fifteenth Street Presbyterian Church in Washington, D.C., had something to say about that in 1914:

> Dr. Booker T. Washington told the colored people of Burlington, N.J., Sept. 8, 1914, that instead of fighting segregation they had better give their attention to improving their homes, so that white people would not object to living near them.
> The implication here is, that the reason why white people object to living near colored people is because their homes are shabbily kept. Now Dr. Washington knew perfectly well that such was not the case. The objection is not to living near the poorer and lower classes of colored people, but to living near any class of colored people.

For blacks and the whites who supported them in the uneasy peace that prevailed after Reconstruction, the crucial question was how to set things right—to put a stop to the lawlessness in the South and win fair treatment for blacks throughout the country. For many years after the Civil War, these people had put their faith in education. Give blacks a decent education, the reasoning was, and they would be able to fend for themselves in the voting booth, the courts and the job market.

It was this view that brought into existence a large number of secondary schools and colleges for blacks. In 1880 there were 39 of them, mostly founded by missionaries from Northern church groups. By 1915 the number had tripled, and the amount of money put into the effort each year by the four main freedmen's education societies had risen from $315,000 to $1,360,000. But it was not enough, for many blacks were left to the mercy of the wretched segregated public schools operated by the Southern states. Even many of the black colleges were less than adequate. A survey of higher education for blacks in 1916 found that most of the schools were understaffed, meagerly equipped and poorly financed.

Booker T. Washington was a prominent spokesman for black people from 1880 until his death in 1915. As founder and head of the Tuskegee Institute, a college-level school for blacks in Alabama, he advocated a program of what would now be called vocational education as a means of equipping blacks to find useful places in their communities.

Another problem was a running disagreement among people interested in education for blacks over what the goal of the effort should be. Should the training be special, sticking to the basics of reading, writing and arithmetic in order to head the students toward jobs? Or should it feature the same broad array of courses offered to most whites, aimed at making the students full and intelligent participants in the economy and the society?

Onto this scene 15 years after the Civil War came Booker T. Washington, an imposing and articulate black man whose mother had been a slave. He believed that the key to success for a black was the ability to provide a service that the world needed. When blacks could do that, he said, they would take a useful place in society and whites would see that education was in the real interest of the South. As Washington put it, "usefulness in the community where we resided was our surest and most potent protection." Speaking to a mostly white audience in Atlanta in 1895—the speech that brought him national recognition as a black leader—he said: "The opportunity to earn a dollar in a factory just now is worth infinitely more [to a black person] than the opportunity to spend a dollar in an opera house."

To that end, Washington favored a program of what would now be called vocational education. As founder and head for many years of Tuskegee Institute in Alabama, he offered just that kind of program to its black students. As an argument for vocational education, he would tell in his speeches the story of the black college graduate who sat in his tumbledown cabin reading French while his property went to ruin. Washington was a persuasive man who spoke widely about his program. He thereby gained a good deal of support among whites, and came to be the dominant figure in black education for some 30 years.

But support for Washington's ideas was not unanimous, particularly among certain black leaders. They thought vocational education was inadequate for blacks and limited them to work on the assembly line or in farming. A broader education would make them better citizens and better able to fend for themselves in a complicated society.

The chief spokesman for this point of view was William E. B. DuBois, a black man who had received just such an extensive education at Fisk University and Harvard University, and who

William E. B. DuBois, another leading spokeman for blacks, was originally a supporter of Booker T. Washington but came to disagree with Washington's approach to black education. DuBois, himself educated at Fisk University and Harvard University, argued that blacks should be given a broad education to make "manhood," rather than mere technical skill, "the object of the schools."

had also studied in Germany. DuBois was at one time a follower of Washington, but by about 1903 he had decided that Washington was on the wrong track. In that year he published *The Souls of Black Folk,* a collection of essays that included several attacks on Washington's approach to black education. Washington, he said, preached a "gospel of Work and Money to such an extent as apparently almost completely to overshadow the higher aims of life." DuBois set out his own views in an essay titled "The Talented Tenth," stating:

If we make money the object of man-training, we shall develop money-makers but not necessarily men; if we make technical skill the object of education, we may possess artisans but not, in nature, men. Men we shall have only as we make manhood the object of the schools—intelligence, broad sympathy, knowledge of the world that was and is, and of the relation of men to it—this is the curriculum of that Higher Education which must underlie true life.

V. P. Thomas put the argument even more flatly. Writing in *The Crisis* in 1915, he said:

There is no doubt that agricultural and industrial training is one of the needs of the Negro, just as it is one of the needs of every race; but to hold up this one training as practically all the training the Negro in this nation needs is to close the door of initiative to the Negro and put him in the class of the domestic animal that is broken or trained to perform one useful service alone. The theory that an education that is not useful is useless is true; but to assume that the only education that is useful to the Negro is agricultural and industrial is to deny that the Negro is a human being.

Whatever form of education blacks got, it did little to significantly improve their lot. Shut out of the voting process, discriminated against in the job market, terrorized throughout the South and in many other places, crowded into segregated neighborhoods, treated unfairly in the courts, they could be excused for wondering if freedom was an improvement on slavery.

Lynching more than the other abuses of blacks eventually provoked a movement among blacks and the descendants of the abolitionists to do more than talk about securing for black people the rights and the protection that the laws supposedly gave them. Black leaders met at Niagara Falls, Canada, in 1905, to found what became known as the Niagara Movement. They issued a "declaration of principles" that summarized the wrongs felt by blacks and the rights they sought. It said in part:

Suffrage: . . . [Blacks] should protest emphatically and continually against the curtailment of their political

rights. We believe in manhood suffrage; we believe that no man is so good, intelligent or wealthy as to be entrusted wholly with the welfare of his neighbor.
Civil Liberty: We believe also in protest against the curtailment of our civil rights. All American citizens have the right to equal treatment in places of public entertainment according to their behavior and deserts.
Courts: We demand upright judges in courts, juries selected without discrimination on account of color and the same measure of punishment and the same efforts at reformation for black as for white offenders.
"Jim Crow" Cars: We protest against the "Jim Crow" car, since its effect is and must be to make us pay first-class fare for third-class accommodations, render us open to insults and discomfort and to crucify wantonly our manhood, womanhood and self-respect. . . .

Three years later a race riot in Springfield, Illinois—the city where Lincoln had lived—was the trigger for another move. Mary White Ovington, a white social worker, later wrote about it:

In the summer of 1908, the country was shocked by the account of the race riots at Springfield, Illinois. Here, in the home of Abraham Lincoln, a mob containing many of the town's "best citizens" raged for two days, killed and wounded scores of Negroes, and drove thousands from the city. Articles on the subject appeared in newspapers and magazines. Among them was one in The Independent of September 3, by William English Walling, entitled "Race War in the North." After describing the atrocities committed against the colored people, Mr. Walling declared:
    "Either the spirit of the abolitionists, of Lincoln and of Lovejoy must be revived and we must come to treat the Negro on a plane of absolute political and social equality, or [J. K.] Vardaman and [Ben] Tillman [fiercely racist public officials in Mississippi and South Carolina] will have transferred the race war to the North."

On Lincoln's 100th birthday—February 12, 1909—Ovington, Walling and Oswald Garrison Villard (grandson of William Lloyd Garrison and editor of the New York *Post*) issued a call for a national conference on the race issue. Their statement, written by Villard, said:

*If Mr. Lincoln could revisit the country in the flesh, he
would be disheartened and discouraged. . . . The
spread of lawless attacks upon the Negro, North, South
and West—even in Springfield made famous by
Lincoln—often accompanied by revolting brutalities,
sparing neither sex nor age nor youth, could but shock
the author of the sentiment that "government of the
people, by the people, and for the people, should not
perish from the earth." Silence under these conditions
means tacit approval. . . . Hence, we call upon all the
believers in democracy to join in a national conference
for the discussion of present evils, the voicing of
protests, and the renewal of the struggle for civil
and political liberty.*

Many prominent people signed the statement. The conference
was held, then another in 1910. From the second meeting emerged
the National Association for the Advancement of Colored People,
usually known as NAACP with each letter sounded individually.
It stated its purposes as:

*To promote equality of rights and eradicate caste or
race prejudice among the citizens of the United States;
to advance the interests of colored citizens; to secure
for them impartial suffrage; and to increase their
opportunities for securing justice in the courts, education
for their children, employment according to their ability,
and complete equality before the law.*

The NAACP quickly organized programs to improve the job
prospects for blacks and to make life safer for blacks in the South
by crusading against the lynching and lawlessness that were so
common there. To serve as weapons in this work it founded a
magazine, *The Crisis,* and set up a Legal Redress Committee to
fight for blacks in the courts. DuBois became editor of *The Crisis*
and Arthur B. Spingarn (a prominent white lawyer in New York)
chairman of the legal committee.

The Crisis soon became a voice strongly arguing the black
cause. It was a cause that needed arguing even after World War I,
in which thousands of blacks fought—but in segregated units. In
May 1919, six months after the end of the war, *The Crisis* had this
to say about blacks and the nation's attitude toward them:

We return from the slavery of uniform which the world's
madness demanded us to don to the freedom of civil
garb. We stand again to look America squarely in the
face and call a spade a spade. We sing: This country of
ours, despite all its better souls have done and dreamed,
is yet a shameful land.

It lynches. . . . It disfranchises its own
citizens. . . . It encourages ignorances. . . . It steals from
us. . . . It insults us. . . .

We return. We return from fighting. We return
fighting.

Make way for Democracy! We saved it in France,
and by the Great Jehovah, we will save it in the U.S.A. or
know the reason why.

The Legal Committee also soon began to make its weight felt. Within 15 years, Spingarn and the white and black lawyers who worked with him had won three important cases in the U.S. Supreme Court. In one of them (*Guinn* v. *United States,* 1915), the Court overturned the grandfather clauses that let illiterate whites vote when illiterate blacks (or literate ones who did not pass the reading tests administered by white voting officials) could not. In *Buchanan* v. *Warley* (1917), the Court threw out laws that forced blacks to live in separate neighborhoods, usually by designating city blocks as all white or all black. The third case, *Moore* v. *Dempsey* (1923), offered blacks some protection against unfair trials dominated by white hecklers. Five blacks in Arkansas had been convicted of murder. The NAACP argued that the trial had been a farce because of white mobs in the courtroom and around the courthouse and because no blacks were on the jury. The Supreme Court agreed, saying:

The [Arkansas] Court and neighborhood were thronged
with an adverse crowd that threatened the most
dangerous consequences to anyone interfering with the
desired result. The counsel [for the defense] . . . had had
no preliminary consultation with the accused, called no
witnesses for the defense, although they could have been
produced, and did not put the defendants on the stand.
The trial lasted about three quarters of an hour, and in
less than five minutes the jury brought in a verdict of
guilty of murder in the first degree.

The NAACP also began a program to investigate and publicize atrocities committed against blacks. One result was *Thirty Years of Lynching in the United States, 1889–1919,* published by the NAACP in 1919. An investigator in that project was Walter White, a black man who later served for many years as executive secretary of the NAACP. He published in 1929 *Rope and Faggott, A Biography of Judge Lynch.* This NAACP program drew public attention to the hard lot of blacks in the U.S.

Gradually, groups other than the government and the NAACP began to speak up for blacks. Organized labor, particularly the industrial unions in the Congress of Industrial Organizations (the CIO, formed in 1935), had many black members and took pains to include them in its achievements for workers. Going further, it formed antidiscrimination committees to act against injustices to blacks. The Catholic Interracial Council, established under the leadership of John La Farge of the Society of Jesuits, worked to interest Catholics in the problems facing blacks. The Anti-Defamation League and the American Jewish Committee were especially active in the field of civil rights. Even in the South, organizations aimed at helping blacks began to form. An example was the Atlanta Civil and Political League, formed in 1936 with the goals of urging blacks to register for voting and to vote, equalizing the salaries of white and black teachers, getting blacks in the police and fire departments and persuading the city hospital to put black doctors and nurses on its staff.

A notable blow against segregation involved the black singer Marian Anderson. She had gained a reputation in Europe and the U.S. as the best contralto of her time. But in 1939 the Daughters of the American Revolution refused to let her present a concert in Constitution Hall, their meeting place in Washington that was regularly made available to white performers. (The women of the D.A.R. celebrated their ancestors who had fought in the Revolution. All the members were white, notwithstanding the fact that a number of blacks had fought in the Revolution too.) Many people viewed the group's discrimination against Anderson as an outrage. Eleanor Roosevelt, wife of the president, resigned from the D.A.R., and at her suggestion Harold L. Ickes, Secretary of the Interior, responded to the D.A.R. action by inviting the singer to present her recital from the steps of the Lincoln Memorial on

In 1939, the Daughters of the American Revolution refused to let the world-famous black singer Marian Anderson present a concert at the D.A.R.'s Constitution Hall in Washington. Eleanor Roosevelt, wife of President Franklin D. Roosevelt, resigned from the D.A.R. At her suggestion, Secretary of the Interior Harold L. Ickes invited Miss Anderson to sing at the Lincoln Memorial on Easter Sunday. A huge crowd attended the concert. Miss Anderson posed later for this photograph.

Easter Sunday. She did, and more than 75,000 people turned out to hear her.

Very slowly, all this chipping away at the iceberg of discrimination began to have some effect. In places where blacks could vote, significant numbers of them began to make their weight felt. Franklin D. Roosevelt was elected president in 1932 with a fair amount of black support. These black votes for a Democrat signaled a major political change, for blacks had consistently supported Republicans since Reconstruction in appreciation of the efforts the party had made in behalf of the freedmen then.

Roosevelt accelerated the shift in several ways. His New Deal program to stimulate the economy helped blacks as well as whites. He received blacks in the White House and appointed a number of blacks to public office. Eleanor Roosevelt, his wife, numbered several blacks among her friends and publicly supported black organizations.

Somewhat surprisingly, the momentum for serious efforts to gain fairer treatment of blacks came from developments during World War II. It was surprising because the situation on the eve of the war did not look promising. The army excluded blacks from several of its branches, including the air corps and the tank, engineer, signal and artillery arms. No blacks served in the marines, and the blacks in the navy held only menial jobs such as ship's stewards.

Even though the Selective Service Act of 1940 (allowing the government to draft men into the armed services) contained a nondiscrimination clause, discrimination continued. The War Department, which ran the Army, issued a stand-pat statement in 1940:

> The policy of the War Department is not to intermingle colored and white enlisted personnel in the same regimental organizations. This policy has been proved satisfactory over a long period of years and to make changes would produce situations destructive to morale and detrimental to preparations for national defense.

But the situation gradually changed. Eleanor Roosevelt sounded the keynote: "The nation cannot expect colored people to feel that the United States is worth defending if the Negro continues to be treated as he is now." A black army officer became a brigadier general in 1940. In the same year the army decided to accept blacks in the air corps. Beginning in 1942, after the U.S. had entered the war, the Navy Department began assigning blacks to all its jobs and giving some posts as noncommissioned officers. Soon the marines started accepting blacks, and in 1944 the navy commissioned black officers for the first time. During the Battle of the Bulge—the last serious attack by the Germans in World War II—white and black troops served in the same infantry companies for the first time.

On the home front, responding to discrimination against blacks in filling many of the jobs created by the war effort, the U.S. set up a Fair Employment Practices Committee and several states passed fair employment laws. Equal treatment for blacks was beginning to be seen as an idea whose time had come.

The events of the war set the stage for Harry S. Truman, who had become president on Roosevelt's death in 1945, to launch what is now known as the civil rights movement. In 1946 he created the President's Committee on Civil Rights. When the newly appointed members came to the White House to hear his instructions, he said to them:

I want our Bill of Rights implemented in fact. We have been trying to do this for 150 years. We are making progress, but we are not making progress fast enough.

CHAPTER SEVEN NOTES

page 85   "The rise . . . " United States Commission on Civil Rights, **Freedom to the Free,** p. 1.

page 85   "full and equal . . . " **United States Statutes.** Washington, D.C.: U.S. Government Printing Office, annually, vol. 18, p. 335.

page 87   "first-class price . . . " Quoted in *James M. McPherson,* **The Abolitionist Legacy,** p. 300.

page 87   "the enforced separation . . . " Quoted in United States Commission on Civil Rights, **Freedom to the Free,** pp.68–69.

page 88   "Discrimination! . . . " Quoted in *Paul Lewinson,* **Race, Class, and Party: A History of Negro Suffrage and White Politics in the South.** New York: Oxford University Press, 1932, p. 86.

page 89   "Rather than permit . . . " Quoted in *Herbert Aptheker* (editor), **A Documentary History of the Negro People in the United States,** vol. 3, p. 577.

page 90   "I am brought in . . . " Quoted in *Herbert Aptheker* (editor), **A Documentary History of the Negro People in the United States,** vol. 2, p. 31.

page 90   "Another thing—. . . " Quoted in *Herbert Aptheker* (editor), **A Documentary History of the Negro People in the United States,** vol. 2, p. 50.

page 92   "A lynching bee . . . " *James M. McPherson,* **The Abolitionist Legacy,** p. 303.

page 92   "uniting native-born white Christians . . . " Quoted in *John Hope Franklin,* **From Slavery to Freedom,** p. 479.

page 93   "to effect certain reforms . . . " Quoted in United States Commission on Civil Rights, **Freedom to the Free,** p. 84.

page 93   "In the degree . . . " *John L. Love,* **The Disfranchisement of the Negro,** p. 26.

page 94   "Dr. Booker T. Washington . . . " Quoted in *Herbert Aptheker* (editor), **A Documentary History of the Negro People in the United States,** vol. 2, p. 69.

page 96   "usefulness in the community . . . " Quoted in *Herbert Aptheker* (editor), **A Documentary History of the Negro People in the United States,** vol. 2, p. 5.

page 96 "The opportunity to earn a dollar . . . " Quoted in *Herbert Aptheker* (editor), **A Documentary History of the Negro People in the United States,** vol. 1, p. 756.

page 97 "gospel of Work and Money . . . " Quoted in *John Hope Franklin*, **From Slavery to Freedom,** p. 393.

page 98 "If we make money . . . " Quoted in *John Hope Franklin*, **From Slavery to Freedom,** p. 393.

page 98 "There is no doubt . . . " Quoted in *Herbert Aptheker* (editor), **A Documentary History of the Negro People in the United States,** vol. 2, p. 92.

page 98 *"Suffrage: . . . "* Quoted in United States Commission on Civil Rights, **Freedom to the Free,** p. 78.

page 99 "In the summer . . . " *Mary White Ovington*, **How the National Association for the Advancement of Colored People Began.** New York: National Association for the Advancement of Colored People, 1914, p. 1.

page 100 "If Mr. Lincoln . . . " Quoted in *Mary White Ovington*, **How the National Association for the Advancement of Colored People Began,** p. 4.

page 100 "To promote . . . " Quoted in *Langston Hughes*, **Fight for Freedom: The Story of the NAACP.** New York: Norton, 1962, p. 23.

page 101 "We return . . . " Quoted in *John Hope Franklin*, **From Slavery to Freedom,** pp. 478–479.

page 101 "The Court and neighborhood . . . " Quoted in United States Commission on Civil Rights, **Freedom to the Free,** p. 91.

page 104 "The policy of the War Department . . . " Quoted in United States Commission on Civil Rights, **Freedom for the Free,** p. 115.

page 104   "The nation cannot expect . . . " Quoted in *John Hope Franklin*, **From Slavery to Freedom,** p. 599.

page 105   "I want our Bill of Rights . . . " *Harry S. Truman*, **Years of Trial and Hope.** Garden City, N.Y.: Doubleday & Company, Inc., 1956, p. 181.

C H R O N O L O G Y

1619   First shipment of 20 African "negers" to Jamestown, Va.

1688   First known protest against slavery by the Quakers of Germantown, Pa.

1775   America's first antislavery society founded by the Pennsylvania Friends (Quakers)

1777   Vermont becomes the first state to abolish slavery

1793   First Fugitive Slave Act supporting the recapture of slaves escaping to freedom

1814   An antislavery society formed in the South (by Quakers in Tennessee)

1817   American Colonization Society founded to resettle free blacks in Africa

1820   The Missouri Compromise seeks to settle the question of expanding slavery to new territories

1822   Liberia founded in Africa for the resettlement of free blacks

1829   Publication of *Walker's Appeal*

1831   Nat Turner's Revolt.

William Lloyd Garrison begins publication of *The Liberator*

1833   Prudence Crandall's school founded

American Antislavery Society founded

1837   Elijah Lovejoy killed

1850   Another compromise attempted on the expansion of slavery

1851   *Uncle Tom's Cabin* published in weekly installments

1854   Kansas-Nebraska Act

Republican Party formed

1856	Representative Preston S. Brooks attacks Senator Charles Sumner in Senate chamber
1859	John Brown's raid
1860	South Carolina is first state to secede from the Union
1861	Confederate States of America formed
	Confederates attack Fort Sumter; Civil War begins
1863	Emancipation Proclamation
1865	Civil War ends; Reconstruction begins
	Slavery abolished by 13th Amendment
1868	Rights of citizens set forth in 14th Amendment
1870	Right of blacks to vote stated in 15th Amendment
1877	Reconstruction ends
1881	First Jim Crow law (Tennessee)
1890	First poll tax (Mississippi)
1898	First grandfather clause (Louisiana)
1910	National Association for the Advancement of Colored People (NAACP) founded
1912	First residential segregation laws adopted
1915	U.S. Supreme Court overturns grandfather clause; first of several cases pressed by NAACP
	Revival of Ku Klux Klan
1919	Peak of interracial strife with 25 race riots
1928	Oscar DePriest of Chicago is first Northern black elected to Congress
1933	President Franklin D. Roosevelt's New Deal program seeks to stimulate the national economy for blacks as well as whites
1939	Marian Anderson denied permission to sing in Constitution Hall; Roosevelt Administration invites her to give the concert later from the steps of the Lincoln Memorial

1941   U.S. enters World War II, expanding role of blacks in armed services

1946   President Harry S. Truman appoints Civil Rights Committee

FURTHER READING

Aptheker, Herbert (editor). *A Documentary History of the Negro People in the United States* (3 vols.). Secaucus, N.J.: The Citadel Press, 1951, 1973, 1974.

Berlin, Ira, et al. (editors). *Free at Last.* New York: The New Press, 1992.

Filler, Louis. *The Crusade Against Slavery.* New York: Harper & Row, 1960.

Franklin, John Hope. *The Militant South.* Cambridge, Mass.: Harvard University Press, 1956.

———. *Reconstruction: After the Civil War.* Chicago: University of Chicago Press, 1961.

———. *From Slavery to Freedom* (third edition). New York: Alfred A. Knopf, 1967.

Freedom to the Free, A Report to the President by the United States Commission on Civil Rights. Washington, D.C.: U.S. Government Printing Office, 1963.

Klagsbrun, Francine. *Freedom Now!* Boston: Houghton Mifflin Company, 1972.

McPherson, James M. *The Struggle for Equality.* Princeton, N.J.: Princeton University Press, 1964.

———. *The Abolitionist Legacy.* Princeton, N.J.: Princeton University Press, 1975.

The Pro-Slavery Argument. (Reprint of 1852 work.) New York: Negro University Press, 1968.

Stampp, Kenneth M. *The Peculiar Institution.* New York: Alfred A. Knopf, 1961.

INDEX

Page numbers in *italic* indicate illustrations.

D

Dartmouth, Town of (Massachusetts) 12
Daughters of the American Revolution (D.A.R.) 102, *103*
Davids, Tice 51
Davis, Jefferson 67
De Bow's Review 8, 29
Declaration of Independence (1776) 19, 46
Democratic Party 50, 55, 89
Dennis, John Q. A. 12
DePriest, Oscar 110
District of Columbia *see* Washington, D.C.
Douglas, Stephen A. 56
Douglass, Frederick 6, 9, 17, 30, 44, *45*
Dred Scott v. *Sandford* (1857) 57
Du Bois, William E. B. 96, *97*, 100
Durham (North Carolina) *86*

E

education vii, *71*, 94–98, 109
Elliott, Samuel 68
Emancipation Proclamation (1863) 72, 85, 110
Embree, Elihu 22
Emerson, John 57
Emigrant Aid Company 49
Equiano, Olaudah *see* Vassa, Gustavus

F

Fair Employment Practices Committee 105
15th Amendment (1870) 80, 110
First Confiscation Act (1861) 69
First Reconstruction Act (1867) 79
Fisk University 89, 96, *97*
Forrest, Nathan B. 80, *81*
Fort Sumter (Charleston, South Carolina) 66
14th Amendment (1866) 78, 87, 110
Frank Leslie's Illustrated Newspaper 71
Franklin, Benjamin 18–19
Franklin, John Hope 2, 80
free blacks vii, 12, 19–20, 22, 24, 27, 33, 71, 73, 76–77, 109
Freedmen's Bureau 71, 78
Freeman, Theophilus 5
Free Soil Party 55
Fugitive Slave Act (1793) 32, 47–48, 109
fugitive slaves 10, 47, 50

G

Gabriel *see* Prosser, Gabriel
Garrison, William Lloyd 38, *39*, 40, 44, 46–47, 55, 82, 109
Genius of Universal Emancipation 40

George III (King of England) 19
Glass, Carter 88
grandfather clause 88, 110
Grant, Ulysses. S. 67, 82
Grimké, Angelina 42, *43*, 46
Grimké, Francis J. 94
Grimké, Sarah 42, *43*
Guinn v. *United States* (1915) 101

H

Halleck, Henry W. 67
Hammond, James H. 1–2, 7–8, 10, 28, *29*, 30
Hancock, John 20
Harper, William 29, 32
Harpers Ferry (Virginia) (1859) 59, *60*, 110
Harris, Sarah 22
Hayes, Rutherford B. 83
Helper, Hinton Rowan 55
Henry, Gustavus A. 10
Higginson, Thomas Wentworth 38
housing 110
Howard, William S. 93

I

Ickes, Harold L. 102, *103*
Impending Crisis, The (Hinton Rowan Helper) 55
Independent 87, 90, 99
Inquirer (Richmond, Virginia) 57
Interesting Narrative of the Life of Olaudah Equiano (Gustavus Vassa) 3
Interstate Commerce Commission (ICC) 87

J

Jackson, Andrew 46
Jackson, Sarah 13
Jackson Mississippian 30
Jardeau, Eugene 11
Jay, John 19
Jefferson, Thomas 18–19, 65
Jim Crow laws 86–87, 99, 110
Johnson, Andrew 77–80
Johnson, Octave 10
Jones, Maybank 68
Justice, U.S. Department of 90
Justice and Expediency (James Whittier) 44

K

Kansas-Nebraska Act (1854) 49, 56, 109
Kendall, Amos 46
Kennedy, John F. 85
Ku Klux Klan Act *see* Third Enforcement Act
Ku Klux Klan (KKK) 80, *81*, 82, 92, 110